Wareham's Way

BOOKS BY JOHN WAREHAM

Wareham's Way 1983

Secrets of a Corporate Headhunter 1980

JOHN WAREHAM

WAREHAM'S WAY

Escaping the Judas Trap

NEW YORK   **ATHENEUM**   1983

For A. J. W.

ACKNOWLEDGMENTS

I SHOULD LIKE to offer a sincere appreciation to my colleagues at Wareham Associates, but for whose dedication and perseverance I would never have been able to write this book. Special thanks are due to my U.S. chairman, distinguished psychologist Dr. Robert N. McMurry, for his expert advice; to my wife for urging me to put my thoughts to paper; and to my editor Ken Bowden, for his encouragement and good judgment.

I would like to thank the many thousands of people who have completed my firm's forms over the past twenty years. Insights gleaned from this material have provided a rich and unique writing resource.

And, of course, grateful acknowledgments to Crown Publishers for permission to quote from *Endings* by Leon Prochnik; E. P. Dutton, Inc. for permission to quote from *Ambition: The Secret Passion* by Jay Epstein; Penguin Books, for permission to quote from D. C. Lau's translation of Lao Tzu's *Tao Te Ching* and Eric Berne's *Sex in Human Loving*.

How to Foretell the Future

INTRODUCTION, EXPLANATION, AND HEARTFELT APOLOGY

HAD I BEEN A COBBLER I should have learned a great deal about leather and feet. If I'd been a stockbroker I'd have hoped to know about securities and interest rates. Instead, my stock in trade is people, and my job has been to judge them.

Like Macbeth's witches I am an advisor to industrial kings—a modern soothsayer and seer; a psychologist and counselor whose task is to foretell the future of would-be executives who are being considered for appointment to a seat in the corporate court.

Predicting a person's future performance turns upon discovering the pattern in his "preordained behavior." In this respect I am fortunate in being able to draw upon a rich source of information. Whenever my management consulting firm appraises a person we work from (1) an in-depth interview, (2) a complete biography, (3) the candidate's actual past on-the-job performance, and

(4) the Wareham McMurry Appraisal Program, a computerized battery of psychological tests that we have standardized throughout the world. We then measure the resulting profile against the psychometric profiles stored in our computer files. Only after that do we make our predictions.

Half a lifetime in this industry has also enabled me to develop a conceptual framework that makes it possible to assess an overall behavior pattern from mere scraps of information. I am also fortunate to have been trained in these tasks by one of the world's most respected psychologists, the chairman of my firm, Robert N. McMurry, who graduated from the University of Vienna with a doctorate in psychology, attended Sigmund Freud's Psychoanalytic Institute in Vienna, and subsequently joined the Chicago Psychoanalytic Society.

One of the key things my work has taught me is that a very large number of people are compelled by their own unconscious mental processes consistently to reject their own best interests, and to engage, instead, in acts of self-sabotage.

It is in the hope of helping such people to live happier and more fruitful lives that I have written this book.

APOLOGY

I have been warned that making Judas Iscariot the subject of my central thesis may alienate some Jews, Christians, and atheists. Other of my stories may, I suppose, also annoy Buddhists, Muslims, and disciples of big business. That would be a pity, for this is not a religious text of any kind, and I have no special cause to promote or to denigrate.

The story of Judas Iscariot, true or not, just happens to illustrate the problem of "preordained behavior." The Bible is also, of course, a handy source of shared history, and I have, accordingly, used some Biblical stories, from both Old and New Testaments, to make some useful points.

Nonetheless, to any reader offended by my words, I offer my heartfelt apology.

CONTENTS

PART TWO
WAREHAM'S WAY OUT OF THE JUDAS TRAP

PART ONE

THE JUDAS TRAP: WHAT IT IS AND WHY YOU'RE IN IT

Unreality is the true source of powerlessness.
What we do not understand, we cannot control.
CHARLES REICH

1. *Three Winners Who Failed*

> *In their enterprises the people always ruin them*
> *when on the verge of success.*
> LAO TZU

> *Right on the brink of success,*
> *something within me says that I don't deserve it,*
> *and I snatch it away from myself,*
> *by committing crimes.*
> DAVID BEGELMAN
> Former president, Columbia Pictures

"LET'S HAVE BREAKFAST, and after that I'll drive you to the airport," said the exiled emperor, purring down the phone.

"That would be fine," I replied. "See you tomorrow at seven."

They'd called him "The Emperor" in the corporate court he'd commanded for nearly twenty years, until the midnight meeting at which he'd been deposed. But that all seemed a long time in the past now.

He'd been the first of my really great clients. I, along with many others, had admired his verve, his easy grace, his catlike cunning. Then, suddenly, for reasons no one could fathom, his judgment turned to jaundice, his deals to dross, and what had passed for poise began

3

to look like arrogance. And, then, in attempting to cope with his problems he began merely to compound them. Finally, the international board, left without an alternative, had him kicked him upstairs, where, six months later, he had his heart attack. I moved to New York about that same time, so that was the last I'd heard of him until now. And what, I now wondered could this sexagenarian former emperor have on his mind?

Across the breakfast table he looked lean and fit. He chose a light breakfast—orange juice, one poached egg, wheat toast—explaining that, after the heart attack, he'd decided to get into shape, and stay that way. He'd installed a modern gymnasium in his home, where he poured his energy into Nautilus body building equipment, and ran on a treadmill.

The conversation was as light as the breakfast until the second cup of coffee, when his question caught me by surprise. "John," he said, "are you happy, *really* happy, with your life?"

In itself the question is nothing. It is, in fact, a somewhat boring question. Was *I* happy? I was so happy I didn't even need to *think* about the question. I turned the query back to him.

"Are *you* happy, Malcolm?" I asked, looking into the cold eyes above the easy smile. He saw me looking, and the eyes warmed.

"Oh . . . well . . . no . . . ," he mumbled. "But I've *never* been happy, I don't know why. Nothing I've done has ever satisfied me, has ever given me the feeling

4

of *being* successful. . . . You know what I mean?

"But that's all in the past. Now I've got a chance to put a really great deal together and get even with those icy bastards whose cold feet cost me so dearly. God, wouldn't I just love to show 'em! Then, with real money in the bag, I could clean up once and for all. Now *that* would give me real satisfaction.

"But you, John, you've made a handsome living from predicting what people will do with their lives, whether they'll fail or succeed, and what will make them happy. You get paid for thinking about these things, so I wondered whether you might have a few answers for me?"

My solution lay, of course, in getting him to talk about his past, and so for many hours that morning I listened to the story of his life, his goals, his triumphs, and his travails. In consequence, I gradually discovered the identity of the Judas behind the hitherto "unfathomable" failures that had so inexplicably ended his career. Emperor Malcolm himself, it transpired, numbed and guilt-ridden by his own "successes," had unconsciously turned his own once uncannily good judgment against himself. And down he had come.

Looking at him across a Hilton breakfast table I realized that the man who had once been a kind of mentor to me, The Emperor whom I had so admired, had never really existed. Impressed by the fact that he seemed completely in charge of himself, I had merely succumbed to a style. Now, however, I realized that he had never understood what he was really doing with his life, and still didn't. Little wonder, then, that his quest for so-called success—money, status, power, praise, prestige—had consumed him, or that he still felt so insidiously, persistently unhappy that, in point of fact, he really was trapped on a treadmill.

On the ride to the airport in his limousine I pondered the problems of helping people like The Emperor to achieve something akin to real success. That would never be easy, however, for it would entail getting such a person to change his thinking processes. Above all, he would have to change his notions of what constitutes "success."

Looking back along the silver wing of the wide-bodied jet that pulled me up and away from the exiled emperor, my mind turned to another client, whom I'll call Bismarck Sliding II. The pampered son of a famous and very autocratic tycoon, young Bismarck II had inherited the family business, and then set out to prove that he was as good as the old man.

In fact, Bismarck II was, as you might have expected, a naive person, and a hopeless executive. He was also imbued with an unconscious need to fail, which he proceeded to gratify with astonishing speed. No one was able to save him from making "investments" in ventures that he knew that his father would never have even considered. Bismarck's whole *modus operandi* inspired despair. Once when considering the outright purchase of a medium-sized manufacturing corporation

6

he asked me to accompany him and "look over the plant and corporation."

I soon found that he meant exactly what he said. Bismarck hired a small airplane and we both, at considerable risk to life and sanity, proceeded to zoom over the factory. That was the full extent of Bismarck's appraisal. "Looked good to me," he said as we landed. Then he paid the full asking price and acquired the whole can of worms.

Bismarck thought he was engaged in the pursuit of profit. In fact, he was really getting even with Poppa by finding ways to lose *everything*. And he succeeded beautifully. Both the family fortune and its prestigious name went down the drain, as, following Bismarck's bankruptcy, the name of Sliding was stricken from the Social Register so vitally important to the old man.

And then, of course, there was Horatio Hubris . . .

"Ah'm gonna make you put your money where your mouth is."

The narrowed eyes of Horatio Hubris, who'd just raised twenty million dollars of public money were focused upon me. My attention was being directed to an article in which I'd written that the great majority of people live lives that are predestined and, therefore, predictable.

Horatio leaned forward in his chair as his eyes widened. "The question is this," he said. "What kind of person am *I,* and what am *I* gonna do with *my* life?"

I already knew enough about Horatio to realize that

he was your typical tyro from the wrong side of the tracks, and, even as his question betrayed a beguiling innocence, free-floating hostility drifted about his head like cigar smoke.

This was not an appropriate time to relate the entire terrible prognosis. It was, however, the moment to give him some simple yet sound advice.

"Horatio," I said, "you're the kind of person who should, if legitimately possible, take, say, a quarter of a million dollars and put it into some kind of trust fund that *you* can't get *your* hands on. You should do this because you're the sort of person who will always *want* to put every last cent at risk. God forbid that it should ever happen, of course, but it is more likely than you might think that you may lose all of the wonderful money that the American people have so eagerly entrusted to your custody. If that ever happens, you'll be comforted to know that the future of your loved ones has been, to some extent anyway, assured."

The announcement, two years later, of Horatio's bankruptcy came as no particular surprise to me. Mildly intriguing, however, was the revelation that Horatio had failed to lay away any nest egg. Instead, he had made, he told me, a "conscious decision" that it was "unnecessary for someone like me to take such a precaution."

Believing Horatio was easy. I knew that the pressures that underlie self-sabotage are as subtle, and as deceptive, as they are powerful.

1. *Three Winners Who Failed*

You may, perhaps, have noticed such pressures in your own life. You'll certainly have read of such illustrious cases as those of David Begelman, the movie mogul who, for no apparent reason, turned to forging checks; of John De Lorean, the auto magnate who, according to police allegations, dealt in cocaine; of Judy Garland, who spun her brilliance into ashes; of Ernest Hemingway, who resolved his problems, once and for all, by placing a shotgun into his mouth, and finding a way to squeeze the trigger.

Such tragedies illustrate a pervasive syndrome that, one way and another, affects almost every living person. I call this syndrome the Judas Trap, and the purpose of this book is to explain how it works, why you are in it, and how to become a great deal happier for whatever is left of your life, by showing you a way to get yourself out of it.

2. *The Judas Trap*

*That deed is not well done
which one regrets when it is done
and the result of which one
experiences with a tearful face.*
BUDDHA

"WHAT YOU MUST DO, do quickly," said Jesus.

Judas wiped his mouth, and quietly excused himself from his twelve dinner companions. He ran out into the night to keep a rendezvous with people who wanted the trouble-making carpenter arrested and silenced. After some haggling over a fee for himself, Judas disclosed that Jesus would be in the garden of Gethsemene the next day. Judas also agreed to lead a party of soldiers there, and to reveal Jesus' identity by kissing him.

Judas made good on his word. He delivered the kiss to Jesus, and Jesus to the Romans. The Romans in turn delivered Jesus to the fate he had anticipated.

Judas was not as lucky. He had failed to foresee the effect of his actions on his psyche. Stricken with remorse, he attempted, without success, to return the thirty pieces of silver. Finally, he strew his "blood money'' in the Temple, ran out of the city, climbed a tree, and hanged himself.

Were all these events, including the death of Judas, ''preordained''? If so, did Jesus know about them? His words suggest that he did, indeed, foresee the whole unhappy chain of events, including the death of the thirteenth diner. In consequence, we are left to wonder why Jesus permitted Judas to destroy himself.

As a true friend, Jesus could surely have taken his troubled dinner guest quietly aside, and explained precisely what would happen if Judas ''chose'' to leave the room.

''Just a minute, Judas,'' Jesus could have whispered into the ear of his disciple. ''Don't do it, don't go. You don't realize what you're getting into. Stay here with us. Relax, put your feet up—have another glass of wine, why don't you . . .''

Perhaps Jesus simply believed that a good friend doesn't interfere in other people's lives, even when they feel compelled to follow tragic paths. Or maybe he knew that it's damned near impossible to save anyone from the consequences of his own actions.

The purpose of this book, however, is to show that the demise of Judas had nothing whatsoever to do with divine destiny; that Judas was, in fact, the unwitting cause of his own demise; *that he fell prey to a web of unconscious forces that compelled him to betray both Jesus and—more importantly—himself.*

In the light of what we now know about human

behavior, let's briefly look at Judas and his motivations as a psychologist—or a headhunter—might.

There is clear evidence that Judas was an archetypal "disoriented disciple"—the kind of emotionally dependent person who is routinely attracted to religious cults and their leaders. People like Judas are usually seeking something—and someone—to give "meaning" to their lives. They are attracted to strong, "masculine," self-assured leaders—father figures—who promise to fill a void in their lives.

Less obvious is the fact that the disoriented disciple also envies and even hates his chosen leader, the reason being that the disciple cannot look upon his leader without being reminded of his own shortcomings. This envy is normally masked and repressed, so that the disciple is seldom aware of his own ambivalence. Unconsciously, however, he is on the lookout for signs of weakness in his leader, and, whenever the hero seems less than heroic, the disciple's envy or hatred may then be manifested.

We see precisely this kind of behavior among sports fans who idolize a performer one day, yet delight in jeering at his failures the next. In truth, the fan is jeering at his *own* weaknesses. The fan sees *his* failings in his hero, and hates the hero for revealing the inadequacies that the fan has taken such care to hide. Paradoxically, the fan and the disciple both harbor an unconscious wish to bring down their idols.

Imagine, then, in this light, what must have gone

through Judas' mind as he watched a woman caress Jesus, and bathe his feet in oil. Judas had joined Jesus' cause because he was dependent, weak, and naively idealistic. Judas wanted to save his soul, and that meant saving the poor, too. By all accounts a parsimonious yet mercenary fellow, Judas was elected the first treasurer of the Christian movement, a role he probably took very seriously. Yet now, before his very eyes, the savior of mankind seemed immersed, at great cost, in the pleasures of the flesh.

Judas spoke out. "That oil could be better used to help the poor," he said. Even now, some two thousand years later, Jesus' reply might seem somewhat disingenuous. "The poor will always be with you," he said, "whereas the Son of man will not."

What kind of answer was that, and what was a person like Judas to make of it? Suddenly, his idol was revealed as a mere man with feet of oiled clay. Or so it must have seemed to Judas.

Jesus was no fool. In everything he said we find him to be quick, tough, and wise to the effect he had on people. He doubtless sensed Judas' ambivalence, could guess that it would be only a matter of time before Judas felt compelled to betray his hero. That did not unduly bother Jesus. His knew his own destiny. He may even have assumed that the unconscious needs of his disappointed disciple were part of that destiny.

What is very clear, however, is that *Judas was the victim of his own mental processes*. First, his religious upbringing had almost certainly taught him to anticipate the arrival of a messiah. Second, Jesus seemed—and claimed—to represent the fulfillment of this prophecy. Third, since all Judas' actions are suggestive of low self-esteem, we can fairly safely assume that he followed Jesus out of a sense of personal inadequacy.

Imagine, then, the guilt that Judas must have felt following Jesus' death. He knew that Jesus' crucifixion represented the fulfillment of Scripture. Judas now had to face the possibility—in fact, the near certainty—that Jesus was what he claimed to be. And Judas had *killed him*! Jesus was Judas' hero, his idol, his father figure, his own sense of self-identity—and now he was gone. Left, in consequence, without a script by which to live his life, Judas could conceive of no alternative to suicide.

So the whole tragedy of Judas Iscariot was preordained only insofar as a web of forces inside his own skull compelled him to seek, and then to betray, a person *like* Jesus. It might also be fair to say that Judas betrayed his own life as well, for, had Judas *realized* his own motivations, he might have been able to save his own life with no help from anyone.

Now, two thousand years later, the trap that claimed Judas is still set to claim you and me. Our traumas and tragedies may not be as dramatic as Judas', but that does not make them any less real.

Two key elements comprise the Judas Trap, and, thereby, a great many of our modern dilemmas.

- Failing to be in *conscious* charge of our lives.
- Wanting things out of a sense of inadequacy.

The failure to be in conscious charge of our own lives, coupled with feelings of inadequacy, is, contrary to popular belief, the *normal* state of mankind. We are like actors reciting lines in someone else's play. We delude ourselves into believing that this is our own special "life," and not a predestined drama; that these are our own words and not mere scripts; that we are free to turn tail or change our behavior whenever we want to. That, unfortunately, is rarely the case.

This somewhat saddening thesis is now supported by every important school of psychological thought, from the Freudians right through to Skinner's behaviorists. The few people who escape this condition are the exceptions, not the rule.

Does this thought-provoking state of affairs actually apply to *you,* too? Almost certainly, the answer is yes. The odds that you are truly in charge of your own life are very, very low.

THE TWO PURPOSES OF THIS BOOK

The first purpose of this book is to impart enough information for you to have a true understanding of the predicament that traps so many people from all walks of life—including, I might add, many apparently successful sophisticates.

The second purpose is to show a way out of this dilemma, so that you may be able to find at least a measure of true happiness in a world that is far from sane. Be warned, however, that the way out may involve a whole new way of thinking about life, and, almost certainly, new notions of ''success.''

SUMMARY

The Judas Trap is comprised of essentially two elements:

1. *The belief that our actions are decided by free will.* We think we're in charge of our own lives, but we seldom are. For the most part, we merely respond to programming.
2. *A further constellation of illusions that stems from emotional dependency.* Though childish of their very nature, these illusions nonetheless compel fully grown men and women to pursue essentially infantile pleasures *from which true happiness can never spring.*

For as long as our lives are governed by either of these two elements, we can neither see nor choose our own best interests, and we are compelled, one way or another, to unconsciously sabotage whatever small measure of happiness we might think we have attained.

That, in essence, is the Judas Trap.

The way out of it begins—and *must* begin—with a clear understanding of the web of unconscious influences that puts us in the trap, and keeps us there.

3. *What I Would Have Told Judas*

Show me a hero, and I'll write you a tragedy.
SCOTT FITZGERALD

IF I COULD RENT A TIME MACHINE and go back to that Last Supper and try to persuade Judas not to betray Jesus, my bet is that Judas would argue the point until his feet were planted firmly in the air.

You, however, are more fortunate. You have both the time and the sophistication to weigh words that might release you from a possibly painful "destiny." On that understanding, then, let us proceed.

The first three things I would have tried to tell Judas—and which I'd also have shared with Emperor Malcolm if he'd given me the time—are these:

• *Your own preordained drama is already in motion.* You, however, are unaware that this is so. Let me explain.

We are born with "clean" brains, but, from that moment, every infant experience becomes fused into our gray matter, thereby establishing "preferred think-ing pathways" that, in point of neurophysiological fact, we are compelled to follow, and to repeat.

These thinking pathways are comparable to a com-puter's programming, and *we* can be very accurately likened to programmed automatons *whose earliest programming is the most pervasive and indelible.*

During childhood each of us is dealt, as it were, a unique assortment of computer cards into which our lifetime scripts are punched. Thereafter, when we im-agine that we are living "our lives," the reality of the matter is that most of us are simply following the in-structions punched into our cards, obeying the imprint that has become a part of our living brain tissue.

These cards define our values, our attitudes, our roles, and our relationships with the other characters in the drama. The cards also establish the ways in which the dramas of our lives will end.

Whether *you* will be a rich man, poor man, beggar man, or thief, depends, at this very moment, upon cards that are *already* in your head. Whether the curtain will close upon your triumph or your tragedy has, to a greater extent than you may ever know, already been written.

How so?

• *Your parents programmed your destiny.* In the unre-solved debate as to whether human behavior springs from genetic inheritance or environmental conditioning, one vital fact is often overlooked: *parents provide both*. Obviously we can't do much to change our genetic inheritance. Less apparent, however, is the inflexible nature of the influences that spring from early environmental conditioning.

Virtually every card in your psychic computer pack carries instructions punched in by your parents, and this programming contains the key to your life drama. And, since your parents also immersed you in a specific environment, it was also they who determined the "cultural overlay" that pervades your psyche. Religion, education, friendships, clothes, manners, accent, eating habits, ideas of beauty, truth, and art—all these things spring from the *place* in society into which our parents placed us. Thus the "accident of birth" imposes a destiny that neither prince nor pauper can easily escape.

Parental injunctions merge with the imposed cultural overlay and thereby define, very precisely, not only your character, but also your script, plot, direction, and ending. And, as we shall soon see, even mavericks are merely *responding* to their programming, thereby fulfilling the prophecy that "You meet your destiny on the road you take to avoid it."

To know what is on your psychic cards is to know your destiny. To change that destiny you must change those cards. Before you can accomplish either of those tasks, however, you must first fully comprehend that your behavior—that virtually *all* human behavior—is controlled neither by logic, nor by intellect, nor by whatever you may from day to day believe to be your own best interest. Your behavior and your thinking processes are almost wholly determined by the *values* and the *scripts* that, one way or another, your parents wrote into your psychic computer cards.

● *Any attempt to thwart your early programming provokes anxiety.* Parental injunctions become perhaps the most dynamic—and certainly the most pain-producing—element of our mental equipment: our *conscience*. The conscience is like a master matrix of computer cards that not only forces the automaton to follow fixed patterns of behavior, but also administers punishment in the form of feelings of anxiety and guilt, should the automaton fail to function as programmed.

The saying "A guilty conscience needs no accuser" points up the fact that feelings of guilt are largely self-administered. Nonetheless, they are real, potent, and pervasive; Shakespeare's Richard III observed:

My conscience hath a thousand several tongues,
   And every tongue brings in a several tale,
   And every tale condemns me for a villain.

Of course, since this "voice" functions at unconscious levels, we seldom actually "hear" it. Instead, we experience strange and unpleasant feelings that render us inexplicably uneasy. This is the power that compels us to exchange real living for automated existence, and to pursue all kinds of ''prizes'' that we do not really want. This is also the influence that frequently prevents the robot from closing its fingers when those things for which it has struggled do, in fact, come within grasp.

Let's now see why values and scripts are the absolute master cards within the human psychic computer pack.

4. *Why and How Our Beliefs Control Us*

*I sometimes think we all die at twenty-five,
and after that are nothing but walking corpses,
with gramophones inside.*
GEORGE SANTAYANA

IT TOOK ME NEARLY HALF A LIFETIME to fully realize that *values are the prime determinants of human behavior.* Our values determine our choice of clothes in the morning, our job during the day, our sexual preference at night, the God we choose to worship or ignore—and much, much more.

In essence, the ten things you need to know about values are these:

1. *A value is a belief that has no basis in fact.* A value is a judgment that cannot be proven. No one can *prove,* for example, that abortion, communism, financial success— any beliefs—are either good or bad, right or wrong. How we make such judgments depends entirely upon the values we assign to ideas. And no one can *prove* our value judgments to be better or worse than those of our neighbors.

Thus, even Moral Majority leaders cannot prove the much publicized evangelical assertion that God would rather talk to a Christian than a Jew. In fact, no one can prove that God even exists. As long as we remain believers, however, then God assuredly does exist—at least inside our own heads.

2. *We are slaves to our values.* Consider the elephant, chained to a heavy stake soon after birth so that it cannot stray beyond the circle circumscribed by the tether. When fully grown, the most powerful beast on earth can be fully restrained by twine tied to a stick. *It does not stray because it believes it cannot.*

Like the elephant, we, too, are enslaved by values that compel us to follow fixed paths. In particular, our parentally programmed beliefs about success confine us within circles that we never chose for ourselves, and that soon become ruts. But we seldom try to fight loose, because we "know"—in our unconscious—that we can't.

3. *Values are absorbed unconsciously, and held unconsciously.* We are seldom *told* what values to hold. Instead, we acquire our most basic beliefs by a process akin to osmosis. By observing as children the behavior of parents, other family members, and friends, we quickly learn the ideas we need to hold in order to survive with a minimum of pain. These notions are imprinted into our brain cells, and become the uncon-

scious beliefs that tether us to what, as adults, we see as "reality."

The result is that we rarely—very, very rarely—know why we behave as we do, including even the most celebrated among us. When a television interviewer some years ago asked Edward Kennedy why he wanted to become President of the United States of America, Kennedy first became uneasy and incoherent, then, after a few moments, answered with hazy platitudes.

The reason for Kennedy's uneasiness was that he wanted to be President for reasons of which he was unconscious. Had his mother been present, she might have answered the question with her own earlier observation that "My children were rocked to political lullabies." Thus, the *belief* that he should be President of the United States of America is Kennedy's tether, the master card motivating his automaton. Kennedy was, in in short, trying to fulfill his preordained family destiny—as we *all* are. Despite his decision not to run in 1984, the chances are that he will continue to find his parental programming irresistible—or anxiety provoking—as time goes on.

4. *The most powerful values are those acquired in childhood.* We chain the baby elephant just as quickly as possible because beliefs absorbed during infancy last a lifetime. As we grow older and acquire new value constellations, we may think that the old values have been tossed out. We would be wrong. The old values are

simply *repressed into the unconscious,* where they do two things. First, they continue to shape our behavior without our awareness of what is happening. Second, the disparity between the old and the new values becomes, as we shall see, a source of conflict and guilt.

5. *Our values give us opinions on everything.* You don't need to actually *know* anything to hold an opinion—in fact, the more ignorant the man the more he delights in his opinions on everything. Where do these opinions come from? Obviously, they come from our values. Our values permit us to *manufacture* opinions on any subject, regardless of how little we may know about it. So, in any discussion, we can produce an endless stream of semiprogrammed responses on just about any subject—motherhood, lovers, apple pie, violence, justice, communism, godliness, newspapers, money, art, literature . . . the list truly is endless. Rarely, of course, do these opinions bear any relationship to reality.

6. *We tend to think that our own beliefs are the only beliefs worth holding.* The automaton "thinks" that its programming, and nobody else's, is some kind of holy writ. George Bernard Shaw described the syndrome beautifully when he observed:

We are overrun with Popes. From curates and governesses, who may claim a sort of professional standing, to parents and uncles and nursery maids and

25

school teachers and wiseacres generally, there are scores of thousands of human insects groping through our darkness by the feeble phosphorescence of their own tails, yet ready at a moment's notice to reveal the will of God on every possible subject.

Jimmy Hoffa once remarked, "I may have my faults but being wrong ain't one of them." Where their opinions are concerned, most people feel much the same way—strongly. Sometimes they may hedge a little, saying, "Well, that's my opinion, and I'm entitled to it." In so doing they fail to appreciate that the idea of being *entitled* to an opinion is just one more example of a value belief. Why, after all, should anyone be *entitled* to an opinion?

7. *We feel a need to convert people to our central beliefs*. If Billy Graham is telling the truth, then why is he always shouting? Like so many crusaders, he's raising his voice because he's not certain that what he's saying is true—but he'd be a lost soul if he could not totally believe it. Converting people to his beliefs convinces him that what he's saying *is* true—and that, of course, keeps him happy. This is common to all zealots, propagandists, and professional crusaders.

No one, of course, is keener to produce a new convert than the recent convert. It's like being the subject of a practical joke: our first reaction is annoyance, but then we look around for someone else to trick. The situation can seem more frightening than humorous, however, when an offspring or friend embraces the beliefs of, say, the "Reverend" James Jones or the "Reverend" Sun Yung Moon.

8. *Our values are rarely consistent.* The Africans have a saying "In the beginning we had the land and the white man had the Bible. Then we had the Bible, and the white man had the land." What the white man really had was two sets of values, both of which he conveniently but sincerely embraced at different times of the week—or even the day, or the hour.

Many of our notions are unconsciously acquired from disparate sources, and, accordingly, it is quite normal for *conflicting* value constellations to find a happy haven inside our skulls, without our being aware of the fact.

Accordingly, it is not entirely surprising to find that Karl Marx, the messianic father of "scientific socialism," could devote his intellect to the alleviation of human suffering, yet shun his own son Freddy by actually *giving him away* to working-class parents, to live as a common laborer and die a pauper. (Meanwhile, "humanitarian" Karl tried to pretend that the poor little bastard had never been born.)

Thomas Macaulay saw the paradox a century ago and noted that "If a man should act, for one day, on the supposition that all the people about him were influenced by the religion which they professed, he would find himself ruined by night."

Quite so. No one is more slippery or ruthless than a virtuous person with a mean mind. Sanctimony is great pepper for the eyes of people who espy our little hypocrisies.

9. *Logic rarely changes values.* Pointing to logical flaws in a person's opinions will rarely make him change his mind. That's because you are trying to rearrange programming of which he is unconscious— are questioning the very foundation of his psyche. His programming *compels* him to disagree with you, even though he doesn't truly know why.

People will, in fact, go to war rather than surrender their beliefs to logic, and most wars are, indeed, fought over so-called moral beliefs. We kill for peace, for liberty, equality, fraternity—for the sake of humankind. Remember the line that came out of Vietnam? "To save the village we must destroy it." The "holy wars" that claimed so many lives were about one set of Christian beliefs being worth more than another. Jesus wept.

Of course, if you *can* win the battle for the mind, then you may not need to go to war at all. Consider the Iranian revolution. The late shah of Iran commanded one of the world's mightiest military arsenals, yet he was overthrown by an eighty-year-old religious fanatic wielding only words, Xerox paper, and homemade tape recordings. Khomeini took charge of his people without firing a single bullet—by winning the space between their ears. But he did not do this with logic—he merely swung the Iranians back to their traditional Islamic values. In short, he touched the trigger that made the robot respond to the programming of its parents.

You might think that intelligence, education, and experience would give people the capacity to rethink and remake their values. That is rarely the case. In an argument between "intelligent" people, the protagonists simply proffer increasingly sophisticated rationalizations while never budging an emotional or intellectual inch.

Expecting logic to change values is, anyway, a little naive, for, as I said earlier, values have no basis in fact. We just believe what we want to believe, and we hear only those "facts" that support our beliefs. The "Foxx experiment" is as nice an example as I know of this truly universal human foible.

An auditorium of students listened to what they thought was a lecture by a distinguished authority. In fact, the fellow, "Doctor Foxx," gave a rambling, jargon-loaded speech that was actually meaningless. First his argument was radical, then it was conservative. The final effect was that he said nothing. Later, the students were polled as to the "Doctor's" perspective. The radical students said he was radical, the conservative students said he was conservative. Everyone agreed he had been both impressive and persuasive.

10. *We deceive ourselves—and others—rather than change our values.* In everyday life, we have three quick ways of dealing with the fellow who points out that we are saying one thing but doing another.

(A) *Reach for the elastic tape measure.* Someone said of Lyndon Johnson that "He exaggerates so often he can't tell the truth without lying." Most of us are a little like that. But are we *really* lying? No, not really. What we are doing is invoking a "logical" process—rationalization—that resembles an elastic tape measure, which we stretch and twist in order to make it accommodate anything we want it to. And, because the process of stretching the tape measure is unconscious, we rarely, if ever, realize what we are doing. In consequence, we are very sincere in our deceptions, and may even believe we are holding up the truth for all to see. But it is not *the* truth—it is simply *our* truth.

A *New York Times* interview with John Lennon and his wife Yoko Ono nicely illustrates the point. The couple explained that they were socialists, even though their income ran into millions and they owned several lavish homes plus a private jet. "There is no doubt that we are living in a capitalist world," Ms. Ono elucidated. "In order to change the world you have to take care of yourself first."

But, of course! In order to be good socialists, the Lennons needed to hang onto their capital. The point for us, of course, is that Ms. Ono was undoubtedly telling the truth *as she saw it*. She *is* a socialist—inside her skull.

Or take the case of Elijah Muhammad, who proclaimed himself leader of the Black Muslim movement and, literally, a god upon this earth. When some ungodlike actions were imputed to him, his devout disciple Malcolm X asked the living god to dispel the rumor that he had been impregnating his secretarial staff in very mortal ways. The answer came quickly:

"I am David," Elijah explained. "When you read about how David took another man's wife, I'm that David. You read about Noah who got drunk—that's me. You read about Lot who went up and laid with his own daughters. I have to fulfill all those things."

Ah, ha!

Or, consider Mary Cunningham, a young woman barely out of college and a campus marriage, who joined the Bendix corporation and met its then chief executive, William Agee. She became something of an overnight success with Mr. Agee who, admiring her mind, elevated her position. He appointed her vice-president, and put her in charge of strategic planning. Cynics, questioning Ms. Cunningham's qualifications, raised a furore, culminating in her resignation from Bendix. Then, following a deal that backfired, Mr. Agee was also deposed. In the midst of it all, however, and to the delight of the press, the unlikely couple "fell in love," had their respective marriages annulled, and joined in holy matrimony.

After it was all over Ms. Cunningham explained her "trial by media" thus: "There's a replica of the Pietà [at St. Patrick's Cathedral in New York] and I looked into the face of the Virgin Mary and I saw the incredible pain as she held her son, who had just been through the most incredible embarrassment, the ultimate in being betrayed by everybody. . . . All I could think of was a sense of identification with the pain.''

(B) *Turn off the hearing aid.* An old man who was partially deaf literally turned off his hearing aid whenever he was losing an argument with his wife. Most of us do much the same even though our hearing is perfect. Our minds turn themselves off and the MEGO (''My Eyes Glaze Over'') syndrome commences. We enter a kind of trance, in which the mind simply doesn't hear whatever unwelcome arguments are being proffered.

Research reveals that, when reading correspondence, the brain takes longer to comprehend bad news than good news. The fact is that the brain *always* attempts to reject bad news—including bad news in the form of other people's differing opinions. The paradox, however, is that, before the bad news can be rejected, it must be read or heard and comprehended. This process gives some idea of why we consistently overrate the worth of our judgments.

(C) *Seize the initiative.* If pressed too far, we can resolve the conflict by becoming bellicose. We might even contemplate fisticuffs. Well, I mean, we're entitled to our beliefs, aren't we? How dare you call me a hypocrite! There, you swine, take that!

THE PARADOX OF VALUES

The paradox of values lies in cherishing what we perceive to be a sacred right to hold invalid and conflicting values. We do so because we think our "principles" make us free. Yet, in truth, the opposite is the case. Our values compel us to live our lives in accordance with illusions—*and thereby enslave us*. The final irony is that we will fight, quite literally, for the right to remain slaves.

So, we think we are in charge of our lives, when, in fact, we are prisoners of our preordination. Like the elephant, our beliefs deny us the capacity to perceive the true reality. In consequence, we are tethered to fixed patterns of behavior that prevent us from ever knowing true freedom.

The paradox of values accounts for much human frustration and suffering. When we now add the concept of *scripts,* we can begin to appreciate why our lives are so rigidly predestined.

5. How "Destinies" Are Made

*We have become automatons
who live under the illusion
of being self-willing individuals.*
ERICH FROMM

IT'S A SHORT STEP from values to scripts. A script is an instruction—or a series of instructions—imbedded within a constellation of values.

Script cards define the robot's role and destiny. On these cards is written everything the robot needs to "know" in order to "live its life" in certain ways, and to carry its performance to the preordained conclusion that the programs require.

Most human dramas can be accounted for by comparatively few scripts—and you, dear reader, are almost certainly governed by one of them. If you knew which one was yours, you might be able to change it. And, of course, that's what we're hoping for. But, first, let's see how everything we've examined so far hangs together, using as an example an actual case history.

THE STRANGE CASE OF
JAMES FORRESTAL, JUNIOR

Mary Forrestal, a devout and humorless Catholic, intended that her youngest and brightest son, James, should become a priest. So, from childhood, he was forced to attend mass regularly, kept to a rigid curfew, and forbidden to swear or tell jokes. Whenever he disobeyed his mother her punishments were swift and severe.

However, much to her chagrin, James became a reporter on a local newspaper. Then, three years later—when all but disowned by his mother—he decided to resume his education, first at Dartmouth, then at Princeton, where he was named editor of the *Daily Princetonian,* and voted by his classmates as "Most Likely to Succeed."

In fact, the young Forrestal failed even to graduate. He felt "impelled to do battle with the school's Catholic chaplain over a series of religious issues." Six weeks before graduation he withdrew from the university rather than bow to the demands of a professor he felt had treated him unjustly.

Thus James Forrestal's scripting denied him the prize he had so assiduously pursued. The Catholicism of his mother, not that of the chaplain, had scripted his battles; the unyielding professor was his mother in another disguise.

The lack of a degree proved no impediment on Wall Street, where Forrestal enjoyed a successful and profitable career. His success, however, served only to further embitter his mother. Even on her deathbed she refused to forgive him.

Shortly after his mother's death, James Junior became involved with an attractive divorcee whom he later married, unannounced, in a City Hall ceremony. "I'm committing the mistake called matrimony," Forrestal informed one of his Wall Street associates in a note he left behind at the office on the morning of the marriage. "Unfortunate woman is Josephine Ogden. See you Monday."

In fact, the unfortunate woman came from an eminent family and was "attractive, sophisticated, popular, witty and loved to attend parties." She was, in fact, the exact opposite of Forrestal's dour Catholic mother. Little wonder, then, that he felt he was "committing" marriage.

The marriage failed. Mr. and Mrs. James Forrestal, Junior, stayed man and wife in name only, living in separate rooms—as Mother would doubtless have liked.

In June of 1940, Forrestal's Wall Street reputation caught the eye of Franklin Roosevelt, who offered Forrestal a place in government. Ultimate appointment to the second most powerful office after the presidency, Secretary of Defense, capped his career. The nation approved, and his friends applauded.

The ghost of Forrestal's mother, however, continued to stir uneasily in the recesses of his subconscious. Eventually, her disapproval eroded his sanity.

Forrestal wrote to a friend, with a "joking" explanation of what success in his new role would require: "I shall certainly need," he said, "the combined attention of the entire psychiatric profession."

He was right. He became unable to make even the simplest decisions, picked his scalp raw, and continually talked to himself while repeatedly wetting his lips from a finger bowl he kept at his desk. He also became paranoid: he believed he was being followed and that his telephone was tapped. (These were symptoms of paranoia prior to Watergate.)

Finally, Roosevelt called for his resignation.

Forrestal complied, then attempted, unsuccessfully, to take his life—once by slashing his wrist, once by hanging himself.

Accompanied by several of his friends, plus the renowned psychiatrist Dr. Karl Menninger, Forrestal was flown to the Naval Medical Center in Bethesda, Maryland. Forrestal's biographer Leon Prochnik observed that:

Forrestal's agitation during the flight was extreme. Convinced his enemies were closing in and that he was about to be exterminated, he berated himself bitterly for having turned his back on Catholicism. He had, he remembered, rejected the priesthood, given up church attendance, and married a divorced woman. It was for these reasons, he insisted, that he was now being punished.

Who could doubt it?

On a warm spring evening Forrestal lay in his hospital bed transcribing from an anthology a passage by Sophocles. When he had carefully copied the first half of the poem, he got up, crossed the corridor, and let himself into the pantry kitchen. Then, in bizarre fulfillment of his oft-stated prediction that he would take his life by hanging, he fastened one end of his bathrobe sash to a radiator situated directly below the thirteenth story window, tied the other end around his neck, and jumped to his death.

Forrestal left no suicide note, but, after his death, when his hospital room was examined, the sheet of paper was discovered onto which he had transcribed a part of the Sophocles poem. It was a translation of the mournful chorus from the ancient Greek tragedy *Ajax*. These were the deathbed lines that James Forrestal, Junior, was writing:

Woe to the mother in her close of day,
Woe to her desolate heart and temples gray,
When she shall hear
Her loved one's story whispered in her ear
Woe, woe will be the cry—
No quiet murmur like the tremulous wail
Of the lone bird, the querulous nightingale—
But shrieks that fly
Piercing, and wild, and loved, shall mourn the tale;
And she will beat her breast, and rend her hair;
Scattering the silver locks that time has left her there

5. *How "Destinies" Are Made*

Forrestal never completed the final verse. When he got as far as the word *nightingale,* he laid aside his pen, proceeded to the pantry, and jumped.

6. *The Illusion That Locks the Trap*

> *How amusing it is to see the fixed mosaic*
> *of one's little destiny being filled out by*
> *tiny blocks of events—the enchainment*
> *of minute consequences with the*
> *illusion of choice weathering it all.*
> ALICE JAMES

YOU CANNOT BECOME FREE until you realize that you are trapped. But, because you *seem* to be in charge of your life, you make the mistake of thinking that you *are* in charge of your life. Thus the *illusion of autonomy* prevents you from transforming your automaton into a real person.

Even now, you still probably can't really believe that *you* may be a preprogrammed automaton. "Look," you say, "I can do anything I want, damnit! I am free to quit my job, if I want to. I can go hang-gliding, if I want to. I can burn this book, if I want to."

Like it or not, the hard fact is that you will only "want" to follow your programming. If you have been programmed to pursue risky endeavors, then you might indeed take up hang-gliding. But if your cards tell you to live carefully, then you will almost certainly never "want" to engage in such an activity, nor "want" to quit your job—even though you may believe that you could if you really "wanted" to.

The illusion of autonomy is well illustrated by the behavior of a man whose brain was stimulated by an electrode during an operation. The stimulated area was the one controlling the right arm, and the man raised that arm. When the operator asked him why he did so, he replied: "Because I wanted to."

This is the way the great majority of us live our lives. Our psychic computer cards are like electrodes in our heads, so that our automaton does what it is told, while "thinking" that it is following its own desires.

WHY THE ILLUSION OF AUTONOMY IS SO DIFFICULT TO DISPEL

Four reasons why the illusion of autonomy is inviolable for most people are these:

1. *We have been programmed to believe that we are "free."* From infancy on, we Westerners are constantly persuaded that adults are free to do whatever they want. And, in America at least, a whole industry, the "success" industry, propagates the gospel that the world is our oyster—that we can do or get or be absolutely anything we want, just so long as we want it badly enough and will work hard enough. As a result, our

41

psychic computer cards are riddled with punch marks that convince us, beyond any shadow of a doubt, that we are Free to Do Our Own Thing.

In the West we are also programmed to think ''logically,'' and, since the popular form of ''logic'' tells us that we cannot *really* be automatons, then our brains automatically reject the notion that we are such—*without ever truly contemplating the idea.*

2. *We are free to select the methods by which we fulfill our Scriptures.* Our robot follows its cards in important matters, but, by choosing its own time and place, maintains the illusion that it is making its decisions freely, and that its behavior therefore is the result of free will.

Consider, for example, the Atlanta broadcaster who, during a radio interview with me, queried the validity of the family destiny concept. Seeking to avoid a possibly fruitless argument, I asked him a question:

''What did your father do?''

''Oh, nothing like me,'' he replied. ''He was a Baptist preacher.''

''But aren't you, too?'' I asked. ''Aren't you just commanding the airwaves to preach your own gospel to a much larger audience?''

He paused. ''So I am,'' he replied. ''So I am. And, do you know, I run a talkback show on Sundays and, over the years, nothing has given me more pleasure than when people have called to tell me that they *stayed home from church to hear my show.''*

Eric Berne recognized the phenomenon, and summarized it thus:

> ''Be devoted to your leader,'' says the Nazi father, and the son devotes himself either to his Fascist leader, or to his leader in Christianity or in Communism, with equal fervour. The clergyman saves souls in his Sunday sermons, and his daughter sallies forth to save them singing folksongs with her guitar. The father is a streetsweeper and the son becomes a medical parasitologist, each in his own way cleaning up the offal that causes disease. The daughter of the good-natured prostitute grows up to be a nurse, and comforts the afflicted in a more sanitary way.

Or take the case of Dick Green, a lawyer who took up ocean racing. He was a totally inexperienced sailor, who, as he explained it, ''just happened to hear the calling of the sea.'' In fact, that ''calling'' made him physically sick, and terrified him. But he persisted, worked like a slave (*exactly*!), risked his life, and ultimately won many prizes.

Much later, when asked why he had felt impelled to embark upon such a course, he reached into his unconscious and found out. His father, he recalled, had always been a superb all-around sportsman, and a compulsive winner who would use any method to beat anyone—including his own son Dick. But there was one thing that Dick's father could not do: he could not step on a yacht without experiencing nausea.

So, to become a "winner," just like dad, Dick's automaton chose a sport that enabled him to beat the "father in his head." However, when you look closely, you see that Dick sailed not to win, but *to get even*—in which pursuit he felt compelled to risk his life.

It's worth noting, too, that the senior Forrestal loved to march bemedaled in the uniform of the National Guard, and that his son won the role of secretary of *defense*. Perhaps young James was attempting to do two things: first, to get even with his mother, the "Virgin Mary," who put the fear of God into everyone; and, second, to fulfill the frustrated dream of his father. If that sounds a little too literal, then heed the words of Carl Jung that "Nothing has a stronger influence on children than the unlived lives of their parents." Time and time again, the images of childhood overtake our lives in the most literal of ways. That the image of a bemedaled father would ultimately cause a grown man to unconsciously seek a role that put him in charge of all men similarly attired, is precisely what we should expect.

3. *We mistake rebellion for freedom.* Like so many people, James Forrestal, Junior, mistook rebellion for freedom. In fact, rebellion is just another way of reacting to our computer cards. We simply turn some of them inside out and *then* do what they tell us, which is, of course, just the opposite of the original instruction.

This syndrome is never more apparent than in the

cases of teen-agers who "discover themselves"—and get even—by becoming, for a time anyway, polar opposites of their parents. Children of the clergy become atheists, the industrialist's son discovers communism, and so it goes.

Unfortunately, whenever we turn our cards inside out, we are likely to be punished in ways we never foresaw. Forrestal rejected the script his mother wrote, which was to "Be a good boy, become a saint, and go to heaven." What he failed to appreciate was that the other side of the cards carried an even more demanding role: "Be ashamed of yourself, you little devil, for you'll never be anything now, so drop dead and go to hell." Not a nice script. Not a nice mother.

What *should* Forrestal have done? He should not have wasted his life responding to childhood ghosts. That, however, is easier said than done, for it is virtually impossible to escape the Judas Trap until you understand the nature of the forces that comprise it, and commit yourself to changing—really changing—the whole basis of your behavior.

4. *We mistake unused cards for a new life.* Responding to previously unused sets of cards is a variant of "rebellion." That's why some middle-aged men—and, increasingly, women—suddenly change hair styles, life styles, work styles and spouse styles.

In fact, unused cards, like the cards of rebellion, are usually punched during infancy, with specific instructions as to when they should be activated: for example, "When you are eighteen (or thirty or forty), use this new bunch of cards, or turn the following cards inside out."

Sometimes a person's cards read: "When you are eighteen (or thirty or forty), throw away all the cards in Series A and leave a vacuum." This vacuum must then be filled by a guru, a revolutionary leader, or a religion—any person or group with a new set of programs compatible with an automaton designed to follow orders.

Our cards may also specify when we shall stop functioning altogether. Consider, for example, the words of Mark Twain:

> I came in with Halley's comet in 1835. It is coming again next year, and I expect to go out with it. It will be the greatest disappointment of my life if I don't go out with Halley's comet. The Almighty has said, no doubt: "Now here are these two unaccountable freaks; they came in together, they must go out together."

Mark Twain's birth did, indeed, coincide with the perihelion of Halley's comet in November of 1835, and so did his death on April 21, 1910. But if there is a God, one would have to imagine that he's too busy to be organizing grandstand exits, even for such illustrious grandstanders as Mr. Twain. No, the truth, more likely, is that the simultaneous arrival of Twain and the comet became such an attention-getter for the infant that his cards became engraved with the need to achieve a final "coincidence." So, even though Twain predicted his destiny, he probably didn't realize that he had, in fact, been programmed to seek it. If only he'd known, he might have lived to be a hundred.

The same thing, of course, happened to Forrestal. His cards told him to attain success and then drop dead. Not even one of the greatest psychiatrists of the day, working with all the resources of the most powerful country in the history of the world, was able to reprogram Forrestal's automaton.

MORAL

The *illusion of autonomy* denies us the capacity to reprogram our automatons. Of course, if we could start writing our own programs we would no longer be automatons. Unfortunately, a knee-jerk rejection of the whole "destiny" concept keeps us living automaton lives, making us toil at tasks we never chose, and binding us implacably to the Judas Trap.

SUMMARY

So far we've seen that the framework of the Judas Trap is this:

1. We think that we are living our own lives.
2. In fact, we are enslaved by unconsciously held beliefs.

3. These beliefs are mostly mere illusions.
4. This realization is hidden from us.

We come now to the second part of the Judas Trap, to the spike within the cage. Actually, I've touched upon it already in the case of the young James Forrestal, but let's look closer.

7. *Why What You Think You Want Will Often Hurt You*

THE SPIKE WITHIN THE JUDAS TRAP consists of the infantile illusions that compel us to pursue pleasure in ways from which true happiness can never spring. Let me expain.

During childhood a set of beliefs defining "reality" is stamped, like "master cards," into the infant psyche. These master cards never leave us, and they define *lifelong* patterns of behavior that we "think" we are choosing for ourselves.

The key point is this: the beliefs on these master cards are, for the most part, *mere illusions that spring entirely from our infantile dependency.*

Thus a dependent child's unconscious notions of how the world works become indelibly imprinted into its infant psyche and *compel the child to repeat its infantile behavior for the rest of its life.*

Let's look just a little more closely and you'll quickly appreciate the nature of the problems this can cause.

DEPENDENCY AND THE JUDAS TRAP

The baby in its crib is totally dependent upon its parents for sustenance, shelter, and psychic satisfaction. The child soon discovers ways to change its world, however. According to the responses of its parents, it learns either to coo or to cry.

In psychological terms, the child's behavior is "positively reinforced" whenever it manipulates its world to get what it wants. Two of the most powerful psychic reinforcments we ever know are Mother's gaze and Father's praise. For the rest of our lives we never "forget" the ways in which we *believed* that we *caused* these reinforcements to be manifested. Equally, we never forget the "negative reinforcements" that follow our parents' wrath.

The cynic, therefore, was not far off the mark when he said that man is the animal born of its mother's womb that spends the rest of its life trying to get back in. In the pursuit of "happiness," most grown adults are simply struggling to regain the *preferred position of childhood*. In that way, they unconsciously hope to reexperience the feelings of security and attention they so enjoyed as children. That, of course, is what Casanova was doing in all those beds—though he, of course, would never have been able to believe it.

The grown adult thinks he is engaged in the free, conscious, and *adult* pursuit of happiness. That is merely his central illusion. In fact, *most of his "adult" actions merely mask the infantile approval-seeking behavior of a dependent child.* Then, whenever these actions are queried, he unconsciously reaches for the elastic tape measure to justify his behavior, while denying its true roots.

In our modern Western world, these infantile behavior patterns are now reinforced until the "child" is anywhere between eighteen and thirty or more years old. The problems of emotional dependence are, therefore, chronic and pervasive. Emotional dependence is a prime source of what Erich Fromm has called "the shadows of uneasiness, anxiety and confusion which never leave us." Dependency conjures the illusions that "destine" us to run down paths we never consciously chose, that compel us to seek—and repeat—destructive behavior patterns.

Even if *you* are that great rarity, a totally nondependent person, many if not most of your problems will almost certainly stem from the fact that virtually everyone else around you is. Don't forget, either, that, if you *are* dependent, you may be extremely anxious to deny this fact—especially to yourself.

In essence, then, the dependent child quickly learns

to get what it wants by doing one of two things: cooing or crying—*obeying or manipulating*. Let's see how these two key patterns trail the "adult" for the rest of its life.

WHY SO MANY PEOPLE ARE SO CONFORMIST

People who learn to obey usually spend the rest of their lives conforming. They comprise what Richard Nixon aptly called the "silent majority," and they exhibit the following symptoms:

The need for authority. The conformist wants to rediscover dear old dad in the form of someone able to provide sustenance, shelter, and psychic satisfaction. In return for those goodies, the conformist promises (unconsciously, of course) to love, honor, cherish, and— most importantly—obey. The conformist also offers the kind of God-fearing respect that a child feels for a father with a whip in his hand.

The conformist projects his unconscious need for a father onto presidents and popes, doctors and lawyers, policemen and judges—anyone capable of delivering what used to be "Father's gaze." What this indicates is a deep unconscious wish to find *a head that is higher than his own*. The importance of this syndrome cannot be overstated.

Religious and political leaders have uniformly understood the need to be "looked up to." Accordingly, all through the ages, icons have been placed in the "higher head position," thereby exploiting the need of the masses for a figure to obey. The image of Buddha is commonly rendered as a giant statue. Kings and queens look down on their subjects from thrones and golden carriages. Russian leaders in Red Square glare down from the top of Lenin's tomb at the people who throng beneath them. The pope blesses the Saint Peter's square populace from his high window. Father's portrait is traditionally hung above the family fireplace. And now, of course, we have the great white corporate chief on the top floor of the skyscraper.

Irrespective of whom or what he is bossing, the Big Boss is less a person than a symbol. His values become the values of his followers. They copy his ideas, his clothes, his mannerisms, his quirks. If he is devoted to physical-fitness, like the head of Johnson & Johnson (who really does keep a treadmill in his office), then his followers will run for their lives. If he smokes Havana cigars, so will they. If he is monogamous, they will keep their affairs to themselves.

A hunger for security and structure at work. The need for initiative frightens the conformist into a structured job where, as long as he does what he's told, he can be blamed for nothing. This is why, contrary to popular opinion, most large-company employees *love* rules and regimentation—and also an autocratic boss. When anything goes wrong, it's *his* fault. "Hell, *I* was only following orders."

The fact that our culture also expects males to seem

macho and exhibit qualities of self-reliance, domi-
nance, tough-mindedness, and so on presents a serious
"image problem" for a great many dependent men.
Corporate life can cover the conundrum. One can simply sign up and bask in the overall blue-chip glow.
Being "on the team" *makes* you a success, and that, of
course, makes you look like Mr. Macho Man. Thus the
company tie and cufflinks give meaning *and* strength to
life. This is the brown-shirt syndrome that gave Hitler
such power—except that nowadays they're wearing
white button-downs, and rep ties. J. Paul Getty saw the
paradox. "Going to work for a large company is like
getting on a train," he said. "Are you going sixty miles
an hour, or is the train going sixty miles an hour and
you're just sitting still?"

Such a train also relieves the dependent individual of
the worry of what to actually *do* with his life. Income,
regimen, uniform, role, self-image, security and success all come with the job. In reality, of course, the
conformist usually pays a financial premium for his
security, because the more security a job offers, the less
it tends to pay, as the following list of roles in order of
reward reflects:

Large entrepreneur
Speculator
Business proprietor
Self-employed business professional (lawyer, stock-
broker, etc.)
Employee of small firm

Employee of large firm
Employee of government
Member of armed services
Member of clergy
    (Does not apply to members of the "electronic"
    clergy: they qualify as entrepreneurs.)
Prison inmate
Inmate within maximum security prison

A hunger for off-the-job security. The conformist clings to structure in all elements of his life. In the not so distant past, if he wanted to know how to "win friends" he bought Dale Carnegie's book, or attended a Carnegie seminar, where they told him how to read the book. Today, he attends a "sensitivity" training seminar, pays to be insulted, and comes away with "it."

For "spontaneous" sexual pleasure he studies the joyous works of Doctor Comfort. He eats formula hamburgers at McDonald's. Music and "literature" come by courtesy of *Reader's Digest*. Then, with the time left over, there is the opiate of the people: "Dallas," pro football, and televised religion.

Unconsciously, the conformist hopes that the magic tube will anesthetize his anguished psyche. In fact, it tortures him further. Both the commercials *and* the programs *deliberately* provoke his insecurity, because, in that condition, he is more likely to respond to the sponsor who wants his money, and the network that wants his eyes.

Networks know that viewers develop "loyalty" to silver-haired anchormen who look like Dad. Little wonder, then, that father-figure Walter Cronkite became the world's "greatest" newscaster.

The idea of a "great newscaster" is, on the face of it, absurd, for the thesis therein is that the newsreader is as important as his news, which is patently nonsense. In actuality, of course, the newscaster is much the more important factor to the network, because the news will change tomorrow, whereas Daddy will be back again to satisfy all the kiddiewinks.

A chronic need to manipulate. Bernard Shaw's Professor Henry Higgins asked a wonderful question: "Why can't a woman be more like a man?" His complaint was that women are elliptical, contradictory, indirect, demanding, manipulative, and, in a word, dependent.

Chauvinistic Henry Higgins would not be surprised that among recent best-sellers was a "women's book" entitled *The Cinderella Complex*. "It is my thesis," says the author Colette Dowling, "that personal psychological dependency—the deep wish to be taken care of by others—is the chief force holding women down today. . . . Like Cinderella, women today are still waiting for something external to transform their lives."

Today? But haven't people *always* been like that? What they're waiting for, surely, is what they've always been waiting for: a Professor Henry Higgins to put thoughts in their heads, words in their mouths, and, most of all, *structure in their lives.*

The thing is this: the problem has little or nothing to do with the lack of a penis, but everything to do with dependency. In Henry Higgins' day the vast majority of women, by the dictate of Victorian society, were dependent, both financially and emotionally. Today, whatever ''liberation'' may or may not have achieved, some 90 percent of the American population—men and women—no matter how rich they may be, are still emotionally dependent. And, like that baby in the crib, the dependent person *cannot* directly ask for what he or she wants, so he or she learns to manipulate instead—and develops an entire personality web around this trait. The strands of that web comprise every trick in the book and then some—except, of course, simply asking for, or taking, whatever one wants.

Manipulation *does* work, however, and, whenever it works, the behavioral pattern is reinforced and the skill honed. In consequence, sycophancy becomes a survival skill; the manipulator learns to fawn a living, and, perhaps, even to elevate crawling into a respectable career.

Such a person makes, for example, a wonderful yes-man, because that role is simply an extension of childhood. Now, instead of Daddy, he manipulates his boss. Yes, *Sir!*

Unfortunately, the manipulator who does not also possess a reasonable intellect often imprisons himself, in that both emotional and economic pressures compel him, for lack of talent, to cling leechlike to a sometimes beastly boss. Other dependent men and women become, in effect, slaves within the giant bureaucracies they are too fearful to leave. Some advertising and public relations people—particularly account executives—often complain of having to "prostitute" themselves, and they do, in fact, exchange their "selves"— their charm, their smiles, their glib chit-chat—for money. The culprit, however, is not the job but the individual, who will remain a "prostitute" in any job until *freed of his own dependency.*

A lust for "love." The dependent person thinks he wants someone to fall in love with. In fact, he wants someone to "love" him the way he was loved in infancy. The song says it perfectly: "I want a girl, just like the girl, that married dear old Dad." What this person *really* wants, however, what he *demands,* is attention, pampering, petting, adulation.

Like Elizabeth Taylor, or the late Peter Sellers, such people are forever destined to vainly seek the perfect mate. The quest *must* end in disappointment *because it is based upon an infantile illusion.* Such people think they are looking for romantic love, whereas, in fact, they are really seeking their idealized parents.

THE ANGRY CHILD BEHIND THE MACHO MASK

The other side of charm is anger, and some very dependent people—usually men—mask their weaknesses by continually running in a tantrum mode. This is the make-up of many a compulsive winner—the person who intends to "get what he wants" at any cost.

Such a person often looks and sounds like an archetypal, self-reliant, highly macho go-getter, and he may, in his conscious mind, even delude himself that he is just that. Behind the burning mask, however, is often to be found an angry and anguished child, full of destructive and self-destructive tendencies.

The chairman of McDonald's, Ray Kroc, seems to have made the kind of remark indicative of this kind of dependency. "It's ridiculous to call this an industry," he is reported to have said, referring, apparently, to his competitors. "This is not. This is rat eat rat, dog eat dog. I'll kill them, and I'm going to kill them before they kill me. You're talking about the American way of survival of the fittest."

In this instance, Mr. Kroc's own choice of words probably signals nothing more than fierce and justifiable pride concerning the content of his corporate hamburgers. Nonetheless, this is the *kind* of remark that tends to typify the deeply dependent overachiever.

THE SYNDROME OF "THE BIG SHOT"

The compulsive attention-getter *needs* approval so badly that he often resorts to limelight-stealing ploys that are both childish and self-defeating.

Consider the emotionally dependent corporate executive. No matter how intelligent and sophisticated he may be, his dependency renders him indecisive and incompetent under pressure. His infantilism also gives rise to childish cravings for status, attention, power, and money—he wants to be a "Big Shot." So, with child-like charm—plus, often, a little treachery—he wins promotion to a top-dog role. Then, of course, poor fellow, his mind reels, his stomach turns, and his life becomes a misery, for now, suddenly, it is not enough to *look* the part; *now he must execute the task*—and continue to do so. Actually *doing* the job, however, is beyond him. So, now, however will he cope?

He usually copes by finding a childish way out of his problems. He tries to distract people, either by charming them or, if that fails, by throwing a tantrum. Alternatively, he may function with one eye on the task and the other looking about for someone to do the job for him—just so long as he continues to get the credit. He is, in short, out of control, and the "crowning achievements" to which his life is dedicated can only bring him increasing pain. It is hardly surprising that such individuals do, indeed, often come very close to suicide.

The ill-fated auto "magnate," John De Lorean, whose life and style seem to exhibit all the characteristics of a tantrum-driven child, is, of course, archetypal. It has been said that De Lorean felt himself to have been "born on the wrong side of town." Such a deprivation would certainly account for the need, apparently, to overachieve, and to project a highly macho image. Accordingly it is not surprising that De Lorean may have been an obsessive body-builder who would release photos of his shirtless torso to the media, and retain public relations people to depict him as a business wizard.

It seems reasonable to speculate that Mr. De Lorean felt compelled to project a "Mr. Perfect" image precisely because, behind the macho mask, he was, in fact, childishly dependent. Iron-pumped muscles, former-model wives, lavish homes, celebrity friends, hither and thither jet-setting, a frenzied need to win, childlike anger—all these things are symptomatic of an identity chronically dependent upon outside approval.

After losing his job at General Motors, the possibly brilliant car designer—and the son of a car assembly line worker—seems to have felt compelled to "show the people in Detroit he could do it." What he *was* able to show, and show very well, was charm enough to attract investment in his "dream car." What he proved, however, was that he could neither effectively manufacture nor market such a vehicle.

Then, according to the police, anyway, De Lorean sought to save face by coping in the way that immature people usually do; by devising an immature scheme. In this case, however, the police allege that his behavior was more than merely childish: for, if John De Lorean really did deal in cocaine without a license, then he committed a criminal offense.

The photos of John De Lorean in handcuffs that appeared in the weekly news magazines might seem to

61

portray a fellow in the pain of poor Judas himself: not in charge of his own actions, not knowing the true causes of his own behavior—a man deeply imprisoned in the Judas Trap. Seen in this light, his own remark, made two years prior, proved prophetic: "I am not a serene person, nor do I have peace of mind. I am not sure how I got the way I am now, but I am driven by a force, and that is not a good way to live."

The personality type that John De Lorean seems so well to exemplify is, in fact, fairly common, and you can quickly spot the type by identifying the following personality traits:

A deep-seated belief in the value of "positive thinking." Strutting about an empty lot, the agitated entrepreneur proclaimed to me: "My new building will be erected on this site by the end of December."

"Of which year?" I enquired, since this was already June.

"You doubt me, or else how could you ask!" he replied. "My building will be erected within the *next* six months, and will be completed by the end of *this* December." Then he railed that his entire life had been hampered by people who lacked his vision, and, most of all, his profound belief in himself. But he had always "showed 'em in the past," and he would "show 'em again now."

He failed, of course. Nobody could have succeeded. To think otherwise was to delude oneself. Yet this fellow did just that—and lost his shirt in the process.

Why? For childish reasons.

The child whose tantrums are rewarded comes to believe that it can get what it wants by yelling. In consequence, it carries delusions of omnipotence into adult life. Then, whenever thwarted, it instinctively grits its teeth and stamps its feet and raises its voice, and engages in what it carefully rationalizes as "positive thinking."

The thing is this. Sure, you must believe in yourself if you are to accomplish anything. And, sure, the world is full of doubting Thomases. And, yes, when you show sufficient self-belief to begin a task, you also dramatically increase the odds that it will be accomplished. But—and it's a big "but"—merely *believing* has changed nothing outside *your* skull. The mountain still waits, impassively, to be climbed.

Hope, all too often, is fear of the present. It is wishing and waiting for Santa Claus—and Santa, you will remember, was merely Daddy in long red underwear. The man who said that you could move mountains, if only you had the faith, also said that you must build your church upon a rock. Oliver Cromwell put it another way "Put your faith in God," he said, "and keep your powder dry."

A fierce desire to compete. Some very dependent people attempt to hide their deficiencies by overachieving and becoming, as they see it, Big Shots. Unconsciously, they seek to regain the preferred position of childhood by beating the hell out of their siblings. In adult life, however, it is their colleagues, friends, and, of course, the competition, that receive their venom. This pattern is especially prevalent among eldest children, and particularly boys. Broadway producer David Merrick put words to the thought that runs through the head of many such a person: "It is not enough that I should succeed," he said. "Others should fail."

People like this live only for appearances, for symbols, for the approval of others, for whatever "celebrity" they think they can win. In consequence, they miss the substance of life itself. They laboriously crack the nut, then throw away the kernel and eat the shell. They believe that all other "capable" people do the same—but can't figure out why the others don't seem to suffer from indigestion as badly as they do.

Oscar Wilde caught the dilemma of such people nicely when he wrote: "There are two tragedies in life. The first is not getting what you want; the second is getting it."

Even those men and women who do succeed in "winning" whatever they think they want, find, much more often than you might imagine, that the game really wasn't worth the candle. They labored under the illusion that they would be happy if only they could build this building, or run this race, or climb this mountain. In fact, the demons that drive them into the Judas Trap often also compel them to release the trigger of the trapdoor through which they then ignominiously depart.

A classic example is Ernest Hemingway. Outwardly Hemingway seemed virile, tough, capable, in charge of his own life. Inwardly he was the precise opposite: totally dependent upon the outside world for approval. He hoped that the "masculine" life style that he took such pains to both live and record would prove that he was a "real man." It was all an act.

In fact, as you might expect if you've stayed with me this far, Hemingway was *really* engaged in getting even with his father, a man who had belittled his son, who fancied *himself* a writer, and who had dreamed of living the outdoor life that young Ernest "chose."

Ernest Hemingway certainly won the fame he sought, and to the casual observer, he seemed to enjoy the kind of life that his father would very much have envied. But it proved not to be enough. The things that Ernest hoped would bring him pleasure, failed, in the end, to fulfill him. Caught in the Judas Trap, desperate and despairing, he finally exploded the myth of masculinity that he had taken such care to cultivate. In 1961, at age sixty-two, he put a shotgun to his head, and, in the most literal sense of the phrase, blew his brains out—exactly as his own father had done before him.[*]

There are many men like Hemingway. Bent on becoming Big Shots, they attempt to "succeed" by "win-

---

[*] Proving, perhaps, the saying that "As a man shoots himself, he also passes the gun to his eldest son." You might note that Ernest's only brother Leicester also became a writer and "outdoorsman." And in 1982, at age sixty-seven, he, too put a gun to his head and killed himself.

ning'' at any cost—a syndrome nicely exemplified by such books as *Winning Through Intimidation*.

The realization that seems to escape the authors of such texts is that no one can ''win'' anything by threatening or frightening or damaging others. It took me a long time to learn, but I eventually did, that unless something is won fairly, then it hasn't been won at all. The reason is that, if you are truly sane, whenever you look at any trophy you didn't win fairly, you suffer remorse—the same kind of remorse that Judas experienced when counting his money.

8. *Why Losers* and *Winners Are Caught in the Judas Trap*

MOST PEOPLE ARE HUNG UP ON WINNING, and, in the looking-glass world behind their eyes, they often have, like the Red Queen, crazy ways of keeping score. These mirror-maze accountings give rise to three basic robot roles: winner, loser, and at-leaster.

A *winner* is a person who fulfills his psychic contract with the world and himself. He sets a goal, commits himself to it, and ultimately achieves it. His covenant or dream may be to run a subfour-minute mile, or write a great novel, or become a professor at Harvard, or direct a great corporation. If he achieves his aim, he is a winner.

If, in the pursuit of those particular goals, a person finishes barely breaking five minutes for the mile, getting published by a vanity house, becoming an EST instructor, or managing a hamburger franchise, then clearly he is a *loser*.

If that person runs the mile in 4 minutes 10 seconds, is appointed associate professor at Yale, becomes a vice-president, or writes a thriller, he could well be described as an *at-leaster*—not a loser, but not a winner either.

The key point is this: whether you will be a winner, a loser, or an at-leaster depends entirely upon *whether you fulfill a contract that exists only in your own head*. That being the case, you may become a legitimate winner simply by running a six-minute mile, playing a tin whistle, holding onto a safe job, or becoming a scout instructor—*just so long as these achievements represent the fulfillment of your own inner psychic contract*.

WHAT MAKES WINNERS, LOSERS, AND AT-LEASTERS

Winners. Parents who want their children to be "winners" usually program them accordingly. Indeed, some parents want the child to win so badly that they don't care whether the effort, or the accompanying psychic contract, causes the robot to break down along the way. When so programmed, a person will set high goals and often attain them—at no matter what cost to anyone, himself included. That's why so many "successful" people ride roughshod over the feelings of family and friends. It's also why so many winners suffer psychogenic illnesses (but, of course, don't like to talk about it, or even have it known).

Losers. We talk about "born losers," but losers are made, not born. Parents who have "lost" often gain perverse pleasure in seeing their own children do the same, and a robot so programmed is thus "destined" to lose at almost everything. Of course, he doesn't consciously set out to fail—and, if he could only think about it, he would not *choose* to fail. He fails because the cards his parents programmed *compel* him to fail. Such a person often talks about winning, and does everything that winning would seem to require. Yet, whenever he gets into a winning position, he finds ways to snatch defeat from the jaws of victory.

Occasionally, by dint of neurotic drive, grim determination, and sheer sweat, a loser may fall upon good times and win the sought-after prize. Then, the accomplishment of the goal so arduously pursued produces anxiety—even, quite possibly, terror. So the loser immediately finds a way to forfeit both the trophy and whatever else came with it.

A dramatic way to do this is to commit suicide immediately after the prize-giving. Novelist Ross Lockridge qualifies on this count. Upon publication in January of 1948, his only book *Raintree County* won him great attention and material reward. Two months later, while six weeks shy of his thirty-fourth birthday, and after six years of labor whose outcome was a six hundred thousand-word manuscript that weighed twenty pounds and took his wife eighteen months to type, Lockridge killed himself.

A variation on this kind of spectacular demise is to suffer public humiliation while *almost* winning. Marathon runner Chris Chataway might have seemed to do this at the 1952 Olympics. After nearly twenty-six miles he ran into the stadium a full lap ahead of his closest adversaries. Four hundred more strides and the prize was his. The crowd stood and cheered him on. The euphoria turned to horror, however, as Chataway stumbled and crawled round the arena, then, only yards from the finishing line, collapsed to his knees and was passed by every runner in the race.

A similar example is that of 1960s middle-distance runner Ron Clarke, who, despite his ability to beat the clock and hold multiple world record times, consistently failed to defeat top competitors, and never won an Olympic gold medal.

Originally programmed to be a winner, James Forrestal, Junior, set and achieved goals that would have pleased his mother, had she not inserted an override card carrying the instruction that any success outside of Catholicism called for Forrestal to be turned into a loser.

At-leasters. There are two types of at-leaster. The first is the robot programmed to be a winner, who, through simple lack of talent, is incapable of achieving his goals. Unable to fulfill its psychic contract, the robot becomes an at-leaster.

Such individuals often suffer from childhood successes that both raise expectations and deny realization that most preadult accomplishment stems from doing what one is told; whereas, in what we call the real world, most of life's real prizes go to the person prepared to break the rules—or to make new rules of his own. Thus the behavior pattern of following orders that makes a child a winner can transform the adult robot into an at-leaster—and the poor devil seldom quite knows what went wrong.

I saw this in a fellow who enjoyed apparently spectacular success at college, but could only rise to a junior vice-presidency at the large corporation he joined in order to save the world. Over lunch he recounted his youthful salad days, then, misty-eyed and gazing blankly over my shoulder, sighed heavily to no one in particular: "I *am* special, I am *still* special."

In fact, he was neither as special nor as well-prepared as the fine sole that lay upon his plate, and, in that moment, I knew I was really hearing the voice of his mother. Mommy had not only dominated him, but had told him that, because he was intelligent and persevering enough to get into a great college, he was "special," and, therefore, destined to greatness. Not so, dear lady, not so. The success never came, and so, to compensate, he married another dominating woman, who keeps him working like a demon—because they need the money to at least *look* like winners.

What *ought* this fellow to be doing with his life? Insight into his own condition could have permitted him to rewrite his psychic contract and start living—*really* living—in the present, instead of looking back over his shoulder all the time while trying to make good on a hopeless psychic contract. In fact, he *wanted* to do just that, and actually dreamed of the simple life for which he was eminently suited. Actually living *that* dream, however, was something that "I could not bring myself to do." No, no, dear boy, Mother would never approve. And the elephant attached to its twine stays in its rut.

The second type of at-leaster has the talent to complete his psychic contract, but is programmed to fail in that task, usually by a competitive father who wants his progeny to fulfill but not surpass him. The psychic cards are programmed accordingly.

Consider the case of a maladjusted dentist. Frustrated that he missed the chance to qualify as a doctor, he nonetheless programmed his son also to be a dentist. When the boy decided, irrespective of Dad's wishes, to become a doctor (a decision probably intended to punish the old man), the father picked a fight and refused to speak to the errant child.

The son enjoyed great success at med school, but "inexplicably" failed to pass his final-year examinations. Obviously, his psychic programming prevented him from seizing the prize he sought. In the end he, too, became a frustrated dentist, just like Dad. Well, that was his destiny, wasn't it? And maybe it was just as well, for he would have been destined to fail as a doctor. But at least he'd given it his best shot, hadn't he? And at least Dad was now talking to him again. But, *of course*.

HOW TO TELL WINNERS, LOSERS, AND AT-LEASTERS BY WHAT THEY TELL YOU

Winners. The compulsive winner constantly quotes people like Vince Lombardi, and has no sympathy with losers. George S. Kaufman observed, for example, that "I'd rather be a poor winner than any kind of loser." Jimmy Carter, who fancied himself a winner, said "Show me a good loser, and I'll show you a loser." Sports agent Donald Dell is on record with the remark, "I can't subscribe to that old cliché that it is not whether you win or lose, but how you play the game. In that case, why keep score?"

Since ambition is the last refuge of the failure, a lot of losers talk this way, too. How, then, do you spot the true winner? Look for a person who accepts the blame for his mistakes and makes a conscious effort not to repeat them: who says, "I made that mistake once, and I won't make it again"; or "It was a costly experience but now we can turn it to our advantage"; or "Now that I see how it's done, that's how I'll do it."

Losers. Losers are compelled to repeat their errors without ever learning from them. Thus a loser is always looking over his shoulder for scapegoats, for ways to assign blame. Also he tends to believe his own deceits. He says, "Yes, but . . ." or "If only . . ." or "I should have . . ." In the role of leader, he says "If it weren't for *them* . . ." If he is one of the team, he blames the leader—and often everyone else, too. To his

73

wife he says "If not for you . . ." to his mistress "If not for her . . ."

An excellent way to spot a loser is to get him talking about his health. Losers like to explain away their shortcomings by pointing to their health: "If it weren't for these damned migraines . . ." and so on, ad nauseam. The loser tends to be a hypochondriac, who if possible, would have his script chiseled onto his tombstone. It would read: "I *told* you I wasn't well." More than this, the classic loser *makes* himself suffer sickness or damage for no good reason. Thus if he can find a good cause, he may become a successful martyr— which is, of course, quite the best way to win by losing.

At-leasters. An at-leaster knows that he hasn't made the grade, and he knows he never will. He realizes— sometimes consciously, sometimes unconsciously— that his contract demands more than he can give, and that it will take all the running he can do just to keep his place on the treadmill. He says, "At least I tried," or "Well, at least I didn't try," or "At least I have this much to be thankful for."

At-leasters are to be found in all walks of life. They are usually quite stable in their relationships, hardworking, and, apparently, quite cheerful. But talk to an at-leaster for long enough and you may well discover the kind of cynicism that masks the frustration of a disappointed idealist.

Many middle-aged Harvard men become at-leasters.

8. *Why Losers and Winners Are Caught in the Judas Trap*

This is because it is extremely difficult to live up to the expectations that a Harvard education raises, in the minds of both the Harvardian and his public. So, at any class reunion, the subject inevitably turns to how those present failed to "realize their potential"—no matter what prizes they may, in fact, have wrested from life. If the party turns to singing, the first song will tell of how we "almost made it."

9. *The Six Basic Robot Roles*

*In reality, killing time
is only the name for another of the
multifarious ways by which time kills us.*
SIR OSBERT SITWELL

AFTER IT HAS BEEN FED, clothed, and housed, the dilemma of the human automaton is what to do with the time before leaving for the Other Place. Daisy, heroine of *The Great Gatsby,* saw the problem clearly. When asked what shall we do this afternoon, she answered "Yes, and tomorrow afternoon, and all the afternoons. . . ."

The answer, for most of the people in the Westernized world anyway, is that they should "succeed." Unfortunately, success in the terms envisioned or alluded to is an illusion. However, we seldom want to be told that. Few of us want to know that there is only life, and us, and just so much time left to enjoy ourselves. This is a thought that many people—most people—find both demeaning and frightening, and so they resolutely block it out of consciousness. Then, in order to fill the days, they simply follow the scripts their parents wrote.

A useful means of identifying various types of automatons is to recognize the ways in which people's programs structure how they use their time in passing across life's stage. These programs lock them in the Judas Trap, making them perform the same basic plot again and again and again, until finally they destroy themselves simply by having failed ever to really live.

If Ecclesiastes was right and there is nothing new under the sun, then our robot roles are already recorded in what we very appropriately call Scripture. So you'll excuse me, I know, for drawing illustrations from that early psychological text.

There are six basic robot programs. They are the Never, the Always, the Until, the After, the Over and Over, and the Limbo.

The Never is a program carried by people whose parents forbade them to take whatever it is that they would most like from life. This is, by definition, a nonwinning program, though some people who look like winners carry it. Moses, for example, though chosen to lead his people to the Promised Land, was condemned by God never to enter it himself. Many apparently outstanding men are caught in the same bind. They are instructed to spend their days Building an Empire, but are forbidden to taste the milk and honey their labors create.

Robots with Never programs seldom can enjoy any

given moment. They are forever saying things like "I can't stay because I've just got to. . . ," or "I'd like to but. . . ," or "Got to run now." And, indeed, they do run—on, and on, and on. A variant is the Never automaton who has all the time in the world to talk about what he would *really* like to be doing, but begins every sentence with "Yes, but. . ." whenever a change of career (or domicile, or life style, or whatever) is suggested.

Tennis player Ken Rosewall seemed stuck in a Never program that compelled him to pursue, but never win, the greatest prize in his sport—the Wimbledon championship. He got to the final many times but seemed never quite able to win. Exactly!

The Always is usually a nonwinning program carried by automatons programmed to spend their lives in single-minded pursuit of a single career. Usually this means Following in Father's Footsteps. It may also mean carrying the same cross he did.

Sometimes, however, the Always automaton is being punished by parents who are piqued that their child chose not to fulfill the standard family destiny. Then onto the psychic cards is punched a damned-for-all-eternity instruction that reads: "If that's what you want to do, then you just go right ahead and spend the rest of your life doing it—and we hope it makes you happy"—which means, of course, "we hope it makes you miserable." So, when the Always automaton isn't rebelling, it often spends a life of quiet desperation Earning a Living—while wishing that it was doing something else. If not most, then many middle-management "executives" are running on Always programs. "But at least," says the Always man, "I've always got my career." Indeed, he has.

The compulsive housewife, Martha, illustrates this script. Jesus rebuked her for failing to realize that there was more to life than getting stuck in a cleaning and worrying mode. In fact, Martha probably enjoyed her telling off. After all, her behavior did catch Jesus' attention, thereby, doubtless, winning Martha a moment of perverse pleasure, in which case she was lucky because very few Always automatons ever find real fulfillment in the roles to which they are bound.

The Until program operates in winners, losers and at-leasters. The Until automaton is programmed to work hard, become deserving, and earn salvation that will come in the form of a special sacrament when the automaton has been made ready to receive it. The sacrament is usually tied to a specific event in the automaton's life. Most professions are worked on this basis. The neophyte lawyer serves years as a drudge, then, when adjudged "ready," he is made Junior Partner—and works even harder. Thus he Makes His Way until, one fine day, he is appointed—wait for it!—Full Partner. O holy and happy scenario! Finally, of course, the blessed automaton gets to sit in judgment as to whether other automatons will be allowed to collect their Untils.

Automatons with Until programs tend to spend their lives Playing The Game; that is, doing whatever is necessary to make good on the Until. What this really means is that the automaton gradually acquires all of the values of the group that can fulfill his Until. This is a pronounced feature of corporate life, where Until rituals are as clearly defined as in any monastery.

Pilate, an Organization Man from way back, was probably running on an Until program. Collecting his Until denied him the ability to set Jesus free, even though he recognized the Nazarene to be an innocent. Like any Until man in such a situation, Pilate simply washed his hands of the matter. Had he not done so, his career might have ended right there.

The Until man carries a psychic calendar against which he measures his progress through life. All Until automatons tend to say "By age thirty (or thirty-five, forty, fifty, sixty, or sixty-five) they should make me a . . ." Winners say, "I was the youngest person ever to be made a . . ." Atleasters say, "Pretty soon now they ought to make me a . . ." The loser says, "They never made me a . . ." Poor bastard.

The After is a nonwinner's program, the premise of which is that pride goeth before a fall, and that having fun presages misery—so Watch Out. An After automaton is raised by voices that foresee trouble in every situation, and say things like: "If you climb that tree, you'll only fall (and hurt yourself.)" As a result, the After automaton continually worries about the rainy day that's bound to be attracted by good weather. He believes that cleaning his car makes dark clouds come. Eating in fine restaurants makes him sick. Pure pleasure scares the heaven out of him.

The result is that After automatons seek maximum job security, and spend a great deal of time making sure they Don't Take Any Risks. Armed with a fat manual, such a person can sometimes become a winner in the role of, say, bureaucrat auditor or banker—anything calling for chronic insecurity, and a dollop of paranoia, and a minimum desire or ability to innovate.

People with After programs love the story of Jezebel, the archetypal good-time girl who came to the stickiest of ends in every way you can imagine. They also like the story of Sodom and Gomorrah, whose people enjoyed such an indecently good time that God decided to destroy their sinful cities. A certain Mr. and Mrs. Lot, however, running on After programs, had foreseen the wrath of God, and taken special care to live Good Lives. God in his mercy gave them time to flee the city, but warned that his retribution would be so terrible that they shouldn't even look back. Mr. and Mrs. Lot had made it up into the hills just as the worst weather that God could conjure struck. So the Lots were all but home free, when, just to gratify herself, Mrs. Lot took a backward peep. Oh, God, what a foolish thing to do! She was, of course, turned into a Pillar of Salt, which is, I am given to understand, a pretty unpleasant way to go. Anyway, the moral, as people with After programs will tell you, is always to be on guard lest some momentary gratification brings the wrath of God down upon *you*. And don't say you haven't been warned.

You can spot a robot running on an After program fairly quickly: it says, "It mightn't seem like a great job, but I'm building up a pension, and at least they can't fire me." Or "She may not be a lot of fun in bed, but at least she is faithful." Actually, I can see an After automaton, out of my window, right now. He's walking up and down wearing a sandwich board that carries his life script on both sides. It reads "Repent, for God's anger is nigh."

The Over and Over is the classic loser's program. Anyone carrying it is destined to fail, over and over and over again. The key parental injunction is that which James Forrestal, Junior, carried to his grave: "You'll fail at everything." It's also possible that Forrestal unconsciously sought to ensure his failure in the next world, too, in that in his mind suicide would certainly have been an unforgivable sin.

A paradox of this program is that the loser tends to spend his life in the pursuit of Get-Rich-Quick Schemes. Riches never result, of course, because the Over and Over automaton is really not looking for ways to win, but for ways to sell himself out and lose. Judas was running on an Over-and-Over program that made him sell his soul for thirty pieces of silver, and then lose that reward along with his reputation and his life.

In Greek mythology the Over-and-Over robot is depicted by Sisyphus, who, you will recall, was condemned to roll a large stone up a mountain. Whenever he reached the summit, however, the stone would roll back to the bottom, and Sisyphus would have to begin all over again.

Over-and-Over people continually tell of how they "Almost made it," and how "It will be different this time." They say, "If only," and "I've changed."

Among the celebrated, Richard Nixon was the greatest Over-and-Over robot of modern times. When he ran for the presidency in 1968 he actually said "I've changed, I'm a new Nixon." For a while he really did seem like a new person. Then came the "accident" of Watergate. And you don't need me to tell you that Nixon both created and refused to destroy those White House tapes because they were his best chance of self-destruction—not just of his presidency, but of his whole reputation. Lyndon Johnson had foreseen it all. "Nixon can be beaten," he said. "He's like a Spanish horse who runs faster than anyone for the first nine lengths and then turns around and runs backwards. He'll do something wrong in the end. He always does." Actually, the saddest remark about Richard Nixon seemed to come from his own mouth. "I'm not a lovable man," he said. He was probably just repeating what his mother had led him to believe.

The Limbo program is really no program at all, but simply the state many people reach at the end of their careers when they retire and are suddenly left with a mind full of blank cards. At such a time the automaton collects a gold watch and becomes an automatic non-winner, even if he'd been a winner up until that moment. The parental instruction that got the automaton this far, "Do what you're told and you'll be a big success when you retire," is not much use when retirement—the Great Until—actually arrives. At that time the Limbo automaton, habituated to a life of time-structuring, must suddenly write its own programs—and no one ever programmed it to do that. So the gold watch really is most appropriate, both as a symbol and as a tool that will be in use almost every moment of every day. Joseph Epstein, writing in *Ambition,* recounts a memorable case:

"Well," said the man, recently retired after selling his eight dry-cleaning shops for something in excess of a half a million dollars, "my day starts off pretty much as it always has. I'm an early riser. So I wake at six, shower and shave. I put on a suit and tie, as I used to do. Some habits you don't change. I don't wake Evelyn. Now that the kids are grown and out on their own, she likes to sleep a little later. I get in the Lincoln and drive to the deli, where I have my breakfast. Now I eat more leisurely than I used to: juice, coffee, dry cereal, a couple of eggs scrambled hard, sometimes an English muffin, sometimes maybe a Danish. I read both the morning papers—see how my stock is doing, check the ball scores, look into the international situation. Sometimes I schmooze a little with Feldman, the owner, whom I've known for years. By now it's about eight-thirty, maybe eight-forty-five. I get back in the Lincoln, pull out of the lot, turn on an all-day news show on the car radio. Then I say to myself, 'Sid, it's not even nine o'clock. How the hell are you going to get through this god-damn day?'"

Limbo automatons spend the balance of their days waiting for Godot, or playing Mahler's "Resurrection" Symphony and hoping. . . . They may get together at reunions and recount old times, saying, "At least we lived a good life and didn't make many mistakes." If there's a record player handy, someone might set Peggy Lee to asking, "Is that all there is?"

Actually the fulfillment of any Until program can leave the automaton with only blank cards, no matter what its age. That is part of the pain of winning at almost anything, and why the automaton that has just made good on an Until often suffers feelings of intense emptiness. It's also why some old men get testy and angry with young people who seem to be enjoying themselves.

10. *What the Judas Trap Teaches*

*Misfortunes one can endure, they come from
the outside, they are accidents. But to suffer
for one's own faults—ah—there is the sting of life.*
OSCAR WILDE

"GIVE THAT TO OSCAR WILDE," said the Marquis of
Queensberry, handing his visiting card to the hall porter
at London's exclusive Albemarle Club, at 4:30 P.M. on
February 18, 1895.

The card bore a handwritten message: to "Oscar
Wilde posing as a Somdomite." Wilde might have
corrected the spelling and returned the card. He might
have laughed and tossed it away. A tortured bore whose
angry visage inspired hilarity, the marquis was seldom
taken seriously—Wilde had dubbed him the "screaming scarlet marquis." And the message was harmless:
posing as a sodomite was an innocuous charge, surely,
to make of a fellow who wore velvet suits, and green
carnations, in 1895.

But Wilde chose to sue the marquis for defamation.

In consequence, he set an epic tragedy into motion.

Lord Queensberry found and paid male prostitutes prepared to testify that Wilde was a practicing homosexual. The ring of truth hung in their tales. On the third day of the trial, when Wilde's barrister realized these tales were to be aired in court, he advised Wilde to drop the case, for, if it went on to the end and the jury found the accusations true, the judge would order Wilde's arrest.

The lawyers guessed that even the withdrawal of Wilde's action might be construed as an admission of his homosexuality, and also lead to his arrest. So they told Wilde he would not be required in court on the final day, during which his lawyers would keep the case going, so that Wilde could leave England. But, despite the forewarning, Wilde refused to flee. Why? This was Oscar's explanation: ''Everyone wants me to go abroad. I have just been abroad, and now I have come home again. One can't keep going abroad, unless one is a missionary, or, what comes to the same thing, a commercial traveller.''

His biographer Hesketh Pearson is less amusing, but very much to the point:

> Despite the pleadings of all his friends, Wilde remained. Having little sense of reality, he could not imagine what was in store for him, and, if partially paralysed by the shock, *he was half-hypnotized by the picture of himself as one predestined to suffer.*

The rest is history. Wilde was arrested and tried,

twice, for the "crime" of homosexuality. The first trial failed to produce a verdict. The second did. Wilde was found guilty and given the maximum sentence—two years with hard labor. The cruel treatment he received in prison ultimately killed him. Despite all of his former wealth, England's most popular playwright after Shakespeare died of cerebral meningitis some thirty months after his release, penniless, in disgrace and exile, in Paris, at age forty-six.

Perhaps, in some ways, Wilde never really left prison. Perhaps his own remark in conversation betrays the truth. "When I was a boy," he said, "my two favorite characters were Lucien de Rubempre and Julien Sorel. Lucien hanged himself, Julien died on the scaffold, and I died in prison."

Was Oscar Wilde "destined" to suffer this fate? Let's look at some of the facts and see what we make of them:

Oscar's father, William Wilde, was, like his father before him, a doctor. Though a grubby little man, William Wilde specialized in aural surgery, upon which subject he became the authority of the day. He wrote several travel books that gained him widespread fame, and he thus became a sought-after lecturer, a role he relished. Fame proved an aphrodisiac, and Dr. Wilde dispensed it freely, for, despite his unwholesome appearance, he enjoyed a special taste for the ladies.

Neither his love of women nor the limelight ex-

tended, however, to the unfortunate events that sur-
rounded the close of his career. Late in life he seduced
an attractive eighteen-year-old patient, and enjoyed a
fairly long-standing affair with her. Then, when he tried
to end the liaison, she sued him. Thus Sir William
Wilde (by then knighted for services to his patients)
became the much-publicized defendant, and loser, of
one of the most lurid court cases of his time.

Oscar Wilde's mother was a revolutionary, a poet,
and a publicity seeker. She regarded herself as a genius.
No one was inclined to argue with a woman of her pride,
or her size.

She wanted a daughter, but, instead, got Oscar. This
fact so disappointed her that she dressed him as a girl
''long after the age when the clothes of male and female
children become distinctive.'' Oscar was pleased by his
mother's strange habits. ''I want to introduce you to my
mother,'' he said to a college friend. ''We have founded
a society for the suppression of virtue.''

He said many other intriguing things, of course, but two
of his remarks are, for our purposes, of special interest.
When asked his ambition in life, he replied: ''God knows!
I won't be a dried-up Oxford don, anyhow. I'll be a poet, a
writer, a dramatist. Somehow or other I'll be famous, and
if not famous I'll be notorious.''

The other remark was made earlier, when he was still
a mere boy and barely out of the frilly dresses his mother
made for him: ''I shall be famous,'' he said, ''perhaps
as an actor, or a dramatist. Or perhaps I will become the

notorious defendant in a wicked court case.''

It does not seem unreasonable to assume that William Wilde's trial had been imprinted on Oscar's psyche, and that he unconsciously—and perhaps sometimes consciously—sought to prove that he was as much a ''man'' as his father, by emulating him and becoming the tragic hero of his own psychodrama. Biographer Hesketh Pearson, who saw the entire tragedy, wrote that Oscar expected the harsh verdict ''because in his fancy it had been preordained.''

And *that,* dear reader, is what I've been doing my best to say from page one. That the whole tragedy *was* preordained. It was preordained *by* Wilde's fancy. He didn't just imagine his destiny—he *wrought* it.

Oscar Wilde became as rich, famous, and immoral as his illustrious father, and as quirky and queer as his mother had programmed him to be. He also fulfilled his childhood dream: he became, as foretold, the notorious defendant in a wicked court case.

But did he get more than he bargained for? If Oscar had realized that unconscious forces were compelling him to destroy himself, would he still have ''chosen'' to sue the screaming scarlet marquis?

And what about you and me? If we knew, *for sure,* that we were embarked upon similar misadventures, would we pass up the chance to waste our lives in prisons or undergo other purgatories of our making? I think that if Wilde had known what you now know he might have torn up that visiting card. But he did not know until too late, and he penned the following lamentation:

> *Strange I was not told*
> *the brain can hold*
> *in a tiny ivory cell*
> *God's Heaven and Hell*

The first point I am trying to make is that whether we live in heaven or in hell is *entirely up to us.* "Heaven, hell, the worlds are within us, man is the great abyss," said Amiel. "Do you not realize," asked Saint Paul, "that God's temple is within you?" The "pagan" tent-maker Omar Khayyám put it this way:

> *I sent my Soul through the Invisible*
> *Some letter of that After-life to spell:*
> *And by and by my Soul return'd,*
> *And answered, "I Myself am Heaven and Hell."*

The second point I am trying to make is that realizing that we have a choice—*truly understanding that there are options*—is the only way to begin making heavens of our brief lives.

The kind of suffering that Oscar experienced is the clear sign of a very bad script. Paradoxically, however, such suffering also carries the seeds of enlightenment. Suffering, better than anything else, can raise our level of awareness, forcing us to question our own behavior, to wonder why we continually get ourselves into difficult situations, and to resolve to mend our ways. In his *trance* Oscar was witty and charming. In his prison cell he became truly wise and wrote, ''At the beginning God made a world for each separate man, and in that world, which is within us, one should seek to live.''

The challenge of life is to gain full possession of ourselves so that we are truly free enough to be able to define our own successes, and to choose our own best interests. When we can do that, we become finally free of the Judas Trap.

How do we do it?

To that task we now turn.

PART TWO

WAREHAM'S WAY OUT OF THE JUDAS TRAP

I don't want the cheese, I just want to get out of the trap.
SPANISH PROVERB

Many of us who walk to and fro upon our usual tasks are prisoners drawing mental maps of escape.
LOREN EISELEY

11. *Reject the Illusion of Autonomy and Realize You're in the Trap*

> *To be a hero one must give an order to oneself.*
> SIMONE WEIL

THE WISEST FILM I ever saw was *The Wizard of Oz*.

You'll remember that the heroine of the tale, Dorothy, played by everybody's sister, Judy Garland, races over the rainbow along with her dog, Toto, in search of the enchanted land of Oz and the wonderful wizard who lives there.

Dorothy is aided in her quest by a tin man who rusts in the rain; a noisy lion who beneath his brave front is terrified of the world; and a scarecrow who can't think straight. Dorothy's attempts to find the wizard are thwarted at nearly every turn by the wicked witch from the west.

At journey's end, however, Dorothy and Toto are

ushered in to meet the wizard. His awesome visage appears on a giant screen; his voice booms from loudspeakers; smoke fills the air. Dorothy, very naturally, is frightened. She is not too frightened, however, to notice strange movements behind a curtain. Then, out of playful curiosity, Toto springs forward and tugs the curtain aside to reveal the wizard. And much less.

Dorothy discovers that, in fact, the wizard is no wizard at all. He is merely a little old fellow furiously manipulating controls to magnify his voice, his image, and his assorted effects.

In this moment Dorothy realizes that she is dreaming, and she begins, in every sense of the word, to awaken. She realizes that she has been in pursuit of an imaginary world: that the land of Oz, and all its characters, exist only in her own head. This realization sets Dorothy free. She escapes from her dream and returns "home," where she rediscovers the wizard and the whole cast of characters. This time, however, she sees them as they really are. She finds that the wicked witch was merely the memory of an unpleasant schoolteacher. The lion, the tin man, and the scarecrow are the imperfect neighbors of everyday life. The wizard is a good-hearted trickster from the local circus.

Dorothy's awakening also brings the realization that *these people comprise, in their way, all there is or ever will be to life.* She sees that it is better to live without illusions than to be chased through life by the ghosts of one's own unconscious. Armed with this knowledge,

Dorothy sets off again on a greater adventure: to enjoy the world as it *is,* and not go dreaming about what may or may not be over the rainbow.

A tragic irony in this whole tale is that the moral of the story, so clear to Dorothy the heroine, seemed to elude Judy Garland the star. She committed the film script to heart, and made "Over the Rainbow" an unforgettable song. She failed, however, to hear the message in her own lines. Judy Garland never adjusted to the real world, failed to find fulfillment, and finally took her own life.

The causes of Judy Garland's particular tragedy lie in an even deeper moral to the whole Oz story. The land of Oz, as any Freudian will tell you, is the unconscious memory of childhood. The wizard is the all-powerful father figure that each of us projects onto an internal screen—and whose approval we seek. The wicked witch is someone standing between Dorothy and the wizard; probably a sister—or a mother—competing with Dorothy for her father's attention. And, of course, Toto, the dog, symbolizes Dorothy's own intuitive processes.

In this context then, it seems likely that Judy Garland never really grew up, that she spent her entire "adult" life trapped in a nightmarish dream. Hollywood, for her, was not so much a place as a state of mind in which she was terrorized, and, finally, frightened to death by characters who, outside of her own head, did not really exist.

The point is that, even though we may think that we are fully awake, we remain in the land of Oz until we realize that we are dreaming. To make that realization we must somehow see behind the scenes, and discover the true identities of the characters who inhabit the land of our unconscious. Only when we permit ourselves to discover the identity of *our* particular wizard, do we begin to awaken.

For it was no accident that Dorothy's awakening began with the drawing of the curtain on the father-figure wizard. The realization that you have been chased through your own life by such a figure is usually the key element in *any* awakening. Consider Terry Trance, for example.

BREAKING THE SPELL ON TERRY TRANCE

"Your ideas may apply to some people," said Terry, "but they certainly don't apply to me." He was disagreeing with an article I had written about family destiny and the illusion of autonomy. To "prove" that he alone was in charge of his life, he related his life story. He punctuated the tale with these words: "So you can see for yourself that it is impossible for my father, or anyone else but me, to be in charge of my life."

Terry had explained that he and his father were not on speaking terms, and had not been for many years. The father, according to Terry, was a man with a "superiority complex, who always treated me like a know-nothing little boy."

Terry paid his own way through college, and earned a first-class degree. But this did not give him the "feeling" that he was "well educated." So, in midlife, he went back to college as a part-time student and completed two more degrees. After that he took up bicycle racing, at which he also excelled.

It seemed a fair guess that Terry had devoted his life to an unconscious competition with his father, and I decided to test the thesis. "You certainly beat your father at being an intellectual," I said. The remark carried the presumption that a game was in progress, and, of course, that Terry was winning. Despite the fact that Terry had denied both of those things, he now nodded his head in agreement.

"I've beaten him at being an intellectual," said Terry, raising his voice, "and I've beaten him at sport. And I'm beating him in business, too." Now Terry's eyes were blazing. "And I'm going to go on beating him," he said, and his fist began to bang his desk, "and beating him, and beating him again!"

Suddenly Terry's illusion of autonomy was dispelled. He realized that he had really returned to college in order to prove that his arguments were as good as those of his father. He saw that he had really spent his life trying to catch his father's attention. Later, explaining why he had wanted to argue the matter, Terry explained that "I like to pick holes in people's arguments, because my father was always so cocksure of himself."

The story shows how difficult it can be to acknowledge the true roots of your own behavior. When Terry, a person of insight and intelligence, was first exposed to the concept of parental programming, his immediate reaction had been to deny that these notions applied to him. It's this knee-jerk rejection of the whole Judas Trap concept—and especially of the illusion of autonomy—that compels us to live automaton lives. That makes us labor under illusions. That hides the truth about ourselves from us.

THE FIRST STEP OUT OF THE JUDAS TRAP

Escaping the Judas Trap is akin to waking from a dream of Oz. *Only when you waken do you realize you were dreaming.*

But, how, if you think you are already awake, can you begin to comprehend that you are really asleep?

The way out of this bind—and out of the Judas Trap—is to make a conscious decision to suspend the illusion of autonomy by accepting and examining the notion that you *might not,* in fact, be fully awake. Suspending the illusion of autonomy enables you to do not one but *two* things. First, to examine the state of your consciousness. Second, to trigger a change in the state of that consciousness.

Deciding to suspend the illusion of autonomy is akin to Dorothy seeing behind the wizard's curtain. Toto's actions merely symbolized Dorothy's own childlike wish to tug at the curtain. And it was not so much looking, but *wishing* to look that triggered Dorothy's awakening, for that decision represented a tentative refusal to accept that things were as they seemed.

The illusion of autonomy is like a magic curtain whose existence is hidden until you decide that it *might* exist. So, even just *contemplating* the curtain's existence triggers the process that will eventually enable you to see the curtain, and then to draw it.

Actually drawing the curtain will, of course, fully dispel the illusion of autonomy, and open your eyes to the realization that you have, indeed, been living a "preordained" life while dreaming.

At that point, you will be *compelled* to acknowledge the existence of another level of consciousness, simply because there is no way around that recognition. And then, of course, you can no longer base your actions upon the belief—the *illusion*—that a thing is true merely because you consciously believe that it is. Now, like it or not, you are pushed into a new *kind* of existence.

SUMMARY

Escaping the Judas Trap involves an awakening process, the first step of which is to reject the illusion of autonomy.

To reject the illusion of autonomy is to acknowledge the existence of a curtain that cloaks the real identity of the assorted demons who have been holding you entranced.

The second step is to actually draw the curtain in

order to discover the wizard, along with the rest of the characters, and the whole goddamned script.

Let's give it a try.

12. *Examine Your Script*

ONE OF LITERATURE'S GREAT IRONIES lies in the story of
Oedipus Rex who hears from the Delphic oracle that he
is fated to slay his father and marry his mother. Shocked
by this prophecy, and determined to protect those whom
he thinks are his parents, Oedipus flees Corinth.

Though unaware of the fact, Oedipus is actually an
adopted child and, therefore, ignorant of the identities
of his true parents. At a crossroad in his travels Oedipus
meets, quarrels with, and kills a "stranger"—in fact,
his own father.

Oedipus subsequently wins the right to become King
and husband to Jocasta, the queen of Thebes. Then,
some years later, Jocasta and Oedipus discover that they
are, in fact, mother and son. Faced with this knowledge,
Jocasta commits suicide and Oedipus blinds himself.

The irony in the tale lies in the admonition inscribed
above the Delphic oracle's door: *Know Thyself* was the

cryptic qualifier to every oracular proclamation. Oedipus failed to heed this warning, and, not knowing his own identity, he was unconsciously compelled to fulfill the oracle's tragic prophecy. In attempting to flee his past, he merely carried it along with him.

Most people do much the same. We are enslaved by the past until we examine it closely enough to discover who we *really* are.

To know thyself, however, is much, much easier said than done, for the very simple reason that self-knowledge is routinely denied to us by our own thought processes. What you *can* do, however, as a highly practical second exercise after rejecting the illusion of autonomy, is *examine your script*.

This means consciously identifying the values, the desires, and the injunctions that have been programmed into your psychic cards. To really know your script is to also comprehend the internal forces that govern your behavior. Once you truly know your own script, you can then set about making a conscious effort to change it—you can choose, for the first time, how to run and live your own life. You may, of course, decide that you *want* to stay "on script"—to live according to your preprogramming. That's fine, too, because, now, even this decision represents your own conscious, autonomous, rational choice.

No one book can, of course, tell everyone everything they need to know in order to discover their scripting. Psychoanalysts making a hundred dollars an hour and up for discovering scripts will tell you that such discoveries take many years. For a reasonably enlightened person, however, a short dose of self-analysis often yields fast insights. Let's look, then, at eleven questions that can definitely help you uncover at least some of your programming. If Oedipus had read these questions he might well have dodged his destiny. See if you agree.

• *What does your family tree tell you?* The apple never falls far from the tree. Families tend to do the same sorts of things, from one generation to another, because their programs get passed on, along with all the other heirlooms. Whether you like it or not, you almost certainly inherited your fundamental scripting from your parents—as, indeed, they assuredly did from their parents before them.

The first questions to ask yourself, then, is who are your parents, and which of them was the most responsible for bringing you up? Parental values are *always* the key elements in any script. To find out what *you* are truly like, you need only study the qualities (and peccadilloes) of your parents. Those same characteristics are almost certainly imbued in you.

The point about Oedipus, as any Freudian will quickly tell you, is that his real parents rejected him during infancy, thereby shaping his entire life. Repressed anger arising from this trauma compelled him to strike out at an apparent stranger, thus killing his father. A happier person than Oedipus would not have done such a thing.

Remember, too, that your parents were scripted to

script you! Accordingly, the person *most* responsible for your programming may well be a grandparent. That person is often a paternal grandmother. You may not even have met the lady in question, but, to the extent that she programmed your father's superego, he will feel unconsciously compelled to implant that same programming in you. In consequence, your conscience—your master set of psychic cards—tends to be inherited from the person who "built" your father's conscience.

In studying your family tree, you can fairly quickly spot your own personality characteristics, and, often, the outline of your "destiny." Religions, attitudes, values, occupations, goals—all comprise the destiny that one generation bequeathes to another.

• *What is your "comfort level?"* The income or status level attained by your family—and, in particular, by your most dominant parent—is likely to represent your own unconscious "comfort level," both physical and psychic.

Your comfort level will almost certainly define the place in the social strata that you will spend most of your life trying to attain—or maintain. This psychic destination is part of the psychic contract that we discussed earlier. If you "arrive" you are a "winner," and if you fail to make the grade then you are, of course, a loser.

You might note that some people from humble backgrounds attempt to erase that perceived ignominy by overachieving, by becoming *visibly* "successful." Such people are, of course, out to "prove" themselves.

The irony, however, is that the further such a person gets from his past, the guiltier he usually feels. Like Emperor Malcolm, such a person hankers for royal "successes" while being, in fact, trapped in the greedy mindset of a serf.

Running upon the treadmill of his own immature beliefs such a person has, in fact, a deep unconscious need—a wish—to end his anxieties by bringing himself down. If he has also inherited a "loser's script"—which is very likely—then the urge to destroy himself may be almost insuperable. This leads, of course, to our next question.

• *Are you a "Winner" or a "Loser"?* When studying your family tree, one of the first things to ask yourself is whether you inherited a winning or a losing script. You can generally guess the correct answer to this question. If you think you inherited a losing script then simply decide, *now,* not to live by it any longer. After all, why should you? Many people stay stuck in loser scripts, yet there is no rational reason for being a loser. British coal miners, for example, have long been "fated" to live miserable lives, and to die of "black lung" and old age, at forty. Why? They go down into hell each day simply because their scripts compel them to do so—as, indeed, did their fathers' before them. If such a person could ever *genuinely* contemplate his predicament, he would almost certainly choose to leave the environment that deadens both his lungs and his mind. In actuality, however, he cannot process such thoughts, and so he can never walk away. Accordingly, he is reduced to complaining, striking, or anesthetizing his psyche in alcohol.

If your own script is giving you a better life than that of the hapless coal miner, you may ask: "Why should I worry whether or not I'm 'fulfilling my family destiny'? If doing so makes me happy, why should I change?"

The answer is that the *mindless* fulfillment of a programmed destiny is *never* truly fulfilling. As long as we are running our lives on other people's programs, we are, whether we know it or not, mere slaves. Or, as Erich Fromm put it, "Whether or not we are aware of it, there is nothing of which we are more ashamed than of not being ourselves." Genuine fulfillment comes from *being oneself,* and from *becoming* the person that one is capable of becoming.

If, after examining your programming, you make a conscious and rational decision that you do, indeed, *want* to fulfill your "family destiny," then that is something else again. The conscious act of reaching that decision dissolves the script. What was someone else's program is now your free choice. You cease to sleepwalk, you stop acting, you start being your true self, you start to live your own life, *you start to become an authentic person.*

• *How do you feel on your birthday?* This question can give you insight into hidden feelings that shaped your early life—and almost certainly continue to shape it right now. Are you the aggressive eldest child who

resented the intrusion of new siblings, and who continues to live with jealousy? Are you the indulged
youngest child, spoilt and dependent? Are you the girl
who was raised to be a housewife and nothing more?
Are you the only girl—the young woman—who was
raised to be a ''success'' *in your father's eyes?* And, if
so, wouldn't you really like to live *your* life by *your*
criteria?

Is it possible you were an unwanted child? If so, is
this fact still affecting you in your adult life today? Who
remembers your birthday? What do they say? How does
that make you feel now? Think about this, and answer
yourself honestly.

• *How did the world look to you when you were a
child?* We live in the past, and the past lives in us.
Childhood's days are preserved in the living brain tissue
that continues to affect our lives. We base many of our
key decisions today upon the past as we saw it then.
Values fixed in infancy are prime sources of ''adult''
desires and repulsions. We choose lovers on the basis of
their resemblance to parental figures. Even as adults,
we remain awed or frightened by the same kinds of
people and situations that scared us in childhood. Until
we take *conscious* charge, our lives are totally governed, in this world now, by feelings we experienced in
that world then. Identifying childhood's demons is the
only way to exorcise them.

• *If a play were written about your early family life,
would it be a comedy, a tragedy, a farce—or what?* Our

early lives become continuing dramas, and we go on playing roles assigned to us by our parents. Are *you* still playing clown, witch, loser, tough guy, Mama's boy— you name it?

Choosing a life of your own entails the realization that you probably spent most of your life playacting in a show that, if you really thought about it, you might not want to keep on the road.

● *What did you have to do to catch your parents' attention?* "It wasn't possible for me to catch my father's attention," said Tom Tycoon. "He was always too involved in his business to be bothered with me." Then Tom remembered that there had, in fact, been one time when his father had shown special interest in him. "It was when I ran away from home," said Tom. "He came after me then."

Suddenly Tom realized something important. "I've been running away from home ever since," he whispered. First Tom left the town of his birth, then the country. Pretty soon he'd lived in some twenty cities all over the world. Only now does he know *why*.

Few people run away from home. Most people, however, are attempting, one way or another, to catch the attention of their parents, thereby recapturing, they hope, the fleeting bliss of childhood love. Why, for example, does a person such as Howard Ruff, well known author, and proprietor of a financial newsletter, suddenly extend his service to include a "hit record" that he made of himself singing "If I Were a Rich Man" and "You'll Never Walk Alone"? Perhaps, in this particular case, Mr. Ruff's sole intention was to exploit his tonsorial talents, and be left singing all the way to the bank. More frequently, however, people who engage in this kind of behavior are like partygoers who seize the bandleader's microphone, thereby exhibiting a deep need for both love and attention.

How you made your parents chuckle can be another key to your programming. The chronic storyteller who feels compelled to tell and retell tired tales is usually chasing his parents' attention. In fact, all approval-seeking behavior—whether of the compulsive winner or the compulsive show-off—reflects just that: a chronic desire for parental approbation. And what is too often overlooked is that many people try to win approval by *conforming*—by living mindless automatous lives.

Only by recognizing our own approval-seeking ploys can we choose to give them up. Until then we are compelled to repeat them.

• *How has the culture in which you live affected your script?* By the mere accident of birth, our parents fix our place in society and then indoctrinate us with the values of that culture. Accordingly, social mores account for much mindless individual behavior.

The Greeks, for example, perceiving Socrates to be a traitor, proffered him hemlock. The Victorians, thinking Sigmund Freud a lecher, pelted him with rotten fruit. A celebrity-infatuated society, sighting greatness in a celluloid idol, elected Ronald Reagan president.

II. *Wareham's Way Out of the Judas Trap*

The Texan who *must* always stay at Hilton hotels around the world may be a joke, but he is, nonetheless, a sad reflection of his conditioning. And, of course, accommodating ourselves in accordance with our social conditioning extends much further than the mere choice of a hostelry. Many people have great difficulty seeing value in anything "foreign," including people.

Our stereotypical Texan in Tokyo thinks he sends out for hamburgers because he dislikes the taste of Oriental food. What is more likely is that he simply cannot *taste* Oriental food. Taste is in our brain cells, and, without established thinking pathways, we are unable, literally, to see the worth in, for example, "foreign" art, "foreign" music or "foreign" religious beliefs. These things are literally like foreign languages to us: until we learn them, we simply cannot comprehend them.

Our parents instill *social* values into us, so that a whole "cultural overlay" becomes part of us, thereby reinforcing most of our key values and, therefore, our life goals, along with our thinking processes. We are normally as oblivious to the social influences that shape our lives as is a fish to the water from which it takes oxygen. We assume that *our* culture is the normal one—and usually also that it is the best one—and thus we take its influences for granted. As anthropologist Edward Hall points out, however, whole societies can, and do, go crazy, and that is part of the reason why so many people "choose" crazy scripts.

• *What happens to people like you?* Intuition is a

wonderful thing. Your answer to this question could be eerily accurate. Even when you're in the Judas Trap, your hunches can often enable you to foretell what "fate" holds in store for you. That's because your fate is already written in your head. If you don't make a conscious change it's likely that you'll "fulfill your destiny." Fortunately, your intuitions can also show you the way out. You can *feel* that something is wrong, you can *sense* what you should really be doing—even if you can't seem to fight the forces that push you in the opposite direction. Study your answer to this question very carefully, then ask yourself if that's what you really want—because you'll get it if you don't watch out.

• *What will your obituary say?* Your obituary *is* your script. It tells who you were, what you did, how well you were liked, and how successful you were. Actually taking a pen in hand and writing your own obituary can be an extemely salutary exercise—particularly if you don't like the look of what you describe. A shortened biography will appear, too, of course, on your gravestone. What would you like that one sentence to say about you? And what, in fact, *will* it say? That you watched a lot of television? That you were one of life's great spectators? That you gave yourself a coronary, but were really a nice guy? That you never quite woke up to the fact that you were alive?

• *Which of your secrets will be discovered after your death?* The truth about a person lies first and foremost in what he hides. An allied psychiatric adage is that "The patient is only as sick as his secrets." That's true, of course, the reason being that our secrets represent much of the gap between reality and illusion. That gap is, of course, one of our prime sources of anxiety.

The beauty of this question, then, is that it makes you focus upon anxiety-provoking secrets that you have suppressed, yet which, paradoxically, you may actually want to bring out into the open.

Freud said that a criminal deliberately leaves clues behind him, because unconsciously he wants to be caught. So do we all. We want to expose even—and perhaps especially—those elements of our lives of which we are most ashamed. Oscar Wilde was asked in court to explain his poem "The Love That Dare Not Speak Its Name." What seems quite likely is that he wrote this poem for the express purpose of having it expose him; that the poem itself represented an attempt, albeit a very elegant one, to publicly confirm his homosexuality.

The irony is that Oscar placed himself in the predicament of having to lie about his secret, in court, in order to reveal it. This is, in fact, quite normal. Where our secrets are concerned, we inevitably want to do two mutually exclusive things: cover them up *and* reveal them. Until they are revealed, we suffer anxiety. In consequence, unconscious forces compel us to find ways of revealing the secret and thereby destroying it—and often ourselves into the bargain.

This is the Judas Trap. Judas felt compelled to sell the secret of Jesus' whereabouts, and thereby destroy his leader. But, without Jesus, there was no life for Judas, for without a guru he was a nobody. That was his *real* secret, and in order to reveal it he hanged himself.

13. *Dispel Illusions That Spring from Dependency*

> *When I was a child, I spake as a child,*
> *I understood as a child, I thought as a child;*
> *but when I became a man I put away*
> *childish things.*
> 1 CORINTHIANS 13:11, 12

THE FIRST THREE OF BUDDHA'S NOBLE TRUTHS are that suffering is the condition of mankind, that the cause of suffering is desire, and that to relieve our suffering we should remove its cause, which is to say that we should surrender our desires.

My own observation is that the cause of most suffering—and one of the key factors that locks us in the Judas Trap—is not so much desire as *infantile* desire, by which I mean desire *predicated upon infantile illusions*.

Such desires and such illusions spring, in essence, from dependency, from an essentially infantile desire to reexperience the bliss of childhood, the warmth of the crib, or the security of the womb.[*]

[*] In our modern world the womb has become a somewhat unsafe place for unborn children, but this realization escapes most people.

116

Similarly, the desire to find a substitute for the parent whose comforting head was sighted at the other end of the cradle causes some people to spend their lives seeking solace from sources outside themselves.

For most people, then, the pursuit of happiness means trying to gratify one of two wishes: (1) the wish to return to the preferred position of childhood, or (2) the wish to find a "higher head" in the form of someone to tell us how to live our lives.

In fact, the gratification of any infantile desire tends to leave us feeling empty rather than fulfilled. Let's look at some examples and you'll see what I mean.

MYTHS THAT LEAD TO MISERY

• *A place will make us happy.* When I was five years old I enjoyed the most wonderful day of my life at a magical beach that glittered beneath the sun as my friends and I played on it. We had so much fun that when night fell I decided I would come back the next morning. That night I set my alarm and dreamed of another enchanted day.

I awoke at 6:00 A.M. and ran off to my Xanadu, only to find that it had faded. The tide was out, the beach was grimy, the day was gray—and none of my friends were around. Suddenly I saw that it wasn't the place that made the day, but my friends and the games we had played. This realization was both a disappointment and a relief. I saw that the place of my dream had not simply vanished, but that it had never, in fact, existed. I also knew, however, that my friends would be at home, kicking around the neighborhood, having fun.

The illusion that a *place* will make you happy is strongly promulgated by, among others, airlines, travel agents, and hotel chains. Want some happiness? Then buy this ticket to Florida, Honolulu, the Riviera—anywhere, except *here*. That's the thing they all agree upon—happiness is *never* here. Well, there's no commission in that, is there?

The illusion is this: we're chasing rainbows looking for a land of Oz that doesn't exist. What we're *really* seeking is the womb or the crib—and the hard reality is that *we will never get back.*

> *This,* right here and now,
> is the only land of Oz
> that we will ever know.
> This, *here, now,*
> is the other side of the rainbow,
> pot of gold and all.
> But we must see it
> for ourselves.

Look, now, over there!—the people of Oz are all about us! They may not be perfect, nor even particularly glamorous, but they are the only people with whom we will ever have the opportunity to be friends. And, if we cannot befriend them, then we will never know friendship. Nor will we ever discover peace of mind.

● *Fame will make us happy.* "If I'm a legend," said Judy Garland, near the end of her tether—and her life— "then why am I so lonely?" Because, Miss Garland, you were looking for happiness *outside* yourself. You were hoping to recapture the attention that you knew as a little girl. Unfortunately, in the real world, fame is no guarantee of happiness. In fact, fame frequently begets misery.

Think of the people who chased and found fame only to discover that in much celebrity there is much sorrow, in much glory there is much grief—Judy Garland, Scott and Zelda Fitzgerald, Ernest Hemingway, Jimmy Hendrix, Janis Joplin, to name but a few. Like moths they flew to the flame, where they found that being "somebody" often involves being reduced to nobody at all. "If you ask me to play myself," said Peter Sellers, "I will not know what to do. I do not know who or what I am." Part of the problem is that fame causes a "personality" to lose its "person" and thus to become a mere commodity. "It's a crazy life," said Nancy Sinatra, talking about stardom. "You're stuck with a product— yourself."

Yet still we live in a world where men and women will literally kill for fame. Immediately after his arrest, Ronald Reagan's would-be assassin (whose name we shall choose to forget) said: "Does this mean I'll be on the six o'clock news?"

A quest for fame cannot, of course, be sated—because no one can get back to the crib. Sure, an audience can applaud, can approve, can scold, just like Mom and Dad used to. But what use is that, if, when the audience leaves, the actor remains a lonely, frightened child?

The kind of fame that comes unsought and unwelcomed is, of course, something else again. Einstein, Schweitzer, and Freud were amused—and perhaps slightly embarrassed—by the fame their work attracted. They knew, however, that real happiness sprang from effort, from accomplishment—not just from fame. When a starry-eyed disciple called Freud a genius, the great man quickly separated fiction from fantasy. "No," he said, "I am not a genius; I have merely made a great discovery."

• *A thing will make us happy.* For years I had admired and lusted to own a rare early model Jaguar. One day I found it in a used car lot. Despite being twenty years old, it was a low-mileage, one-owner vehicle, and it shone like the sun. The interior was real leather—the sort that smells of money.

And money it took to buy it—more, needless to say, than I had bargained for. I demurred for a couple of days because I already owned a very nice car. Finally, I could not restrain myself. I parted with my money, slid into the driver's seat, turned on the ignition, engaged the engine, and began, slowly, to awaken.

I don't know what I had been expecting, but I quickly discovered that it would never be found inside that car. It was heavy and cumbersome on the road, and neither the steering wheel nor the accelerator were responsive.

The pleasure I had so keenly anticipated had vanished. As I rolled away from the lot, I wondered what on earth I had been thinking about and what I was then doing.

Some weeks later, still pondering that question, I looked for an answer in my childhood—and found it right there. My father had been the first man in town to buy a Jaguar car, and that purchase, I remembered, was of some importance to him. A year later he was annoyed to see a new and sleeker model pass him at an intersection. "It's no good," I remember him saying. But the green of envy tinged his words.

So, a quarter of a century later, I tried to buy the car my father had deprecated: the same make, year, and model number—and without really knowing why. I simply felt there was some special "look" to the car. And in some ways there was, because it represented a chance for me to even a score from my childhood.

The older the boys, the bigger their toys. Many of us can and do waste a tremendous amount of our adult lives attempting, one way or another, to purchase adult versions of childhood's toys. The hope we will succeed in this hopeless endeavor springs as eternal as the illusions that clever admen are so highly paid to create, and to endlessly re-create.

On this subject of owning things, Freud observed that all children, before they reach maturity, go through a phase that he called anal-erotic, which is to say that they get pleasure from holding onto their feces, thereby denying it to Mother—and thus getting even with her.

Some people never leave this immature state of development, and develop accordingly what Freud called anal personalities. These are the tightwads whose lives are devoted to "holding on," to having, to saving, to hoarding—money, things, feelings, gestures, words, energy. And, yes, even feces, for hoarders frequently suffer chronic constipation.

What matters, in Freud's view, is that the major orientation toward possession occurs in the period *before* the achievement of full maturity. If it remains permanently, it is pathological.

To put it very simply, owning things for pleasure can be infantile and sick. All we're really trying to do— according to one of the greatest philosophers of our age—is reexperience the pleasure of the pot! Don't laugh. A vast number of people, particularly in America, the world's most materialistic and maternalistic society, are stuck with this problem.

They believe, on many levels, that possessing things will make them happy. And then, of course, the fear of losing what they are holding onto creates anxiety. So even just *believing* that things will make you happy, can, in fact, make you ill.

• *Happiness is behind the green door.* A frustrated fellow once offered to pay me to tell him how to speak like a corporate director. "I'm being held back by not knowing how they talk in the boardroom," he explained. "They talk in ways that I wouldn't be able to understand." Poor fellow. He knew they weren't speaking in tongues, yet he subscribed to this idea of mysterious things happening that were beyond his intellectual capacity.

One of life's greatest illusions is that, somewhere, behind a firmly closed door, an exclusive coterie of beautiful people is enjoying a perpetually wonderful time, doing endlessly exciting and glamorous things. If you ever find yourself thinking anything like this, then look at a transcript of the Nixon tapes. Here, as never before in history, we are made privy to the thought processes and conversations of men locked inside the Oval Office of the White House. What great wisdom can we learn from these great men? What pearls do they offer? To their horror, one hopes, and certainly to our dismay, we find that, shorn of their pubescent expletives, the emperor and all his court are worse than nude—they are downright *ordinary*. Ordinary, trite, and banal. Serves us right for believing they would be anything else.

Often, when we assume that other people—and particularly the celebrated—are infinitely wiser than we are, we're simply trying to get back to childhood, where, behind their bedroom door, our parents "knew what was best for us." That belief, whether it was true or not, made us feel secure. But childhood is *over* now, and to put our faith in surrogate fathers, as many of us are unconsciously compelled to do, is to invite at least disappointment, and, all too often, tragedy.

"Society," said our old friend Oscar Wilde, "to be

in it is a bore, to be out of it a tragedy.'' The extent of the tragedy depends only upon your *need for approval*. Certainly it *can* be fun to go backstage as it were, but it has been my experience all over the world that backstage is merely that: a dusty, tawdry, sweaty nowhere-place where actors mostly worry about remembering their lines and what the audience thinks.

There are, of course, some very nice private clubs that you might like to join. And, in fact, getting in might be easier than you think, because all you have to do is convince the members that you are *just like them*. But then, if you have to wear a mask to join, why bother? The best club in the world could be right behind your own front door.

- *"Winning" will make me happy.* If and when you realize and accept that the compulsive winner is really competing for the attention of his parents, the futility of the exercise becomes instantly apparent. On the other hand, as we have seen, losing can also be a way of winning approval. Is there *anything* we can do, then, that can't be labeled infantile? Yes, of course, there are many things. The point is that neither winning nor losing signifies immaturity *in itself*. It's our *motives* that betray us, as T.S. Eliot points out:

> *The last temptation is the greatest treason:*
> *To do the right deed for the wrong reason.*

But how, you ask, do I know when I'm winning (or losing) for the wrong reason? Be sure that your body and your mind will let you know, *if you will only listen to them*. If, for example, you've beaten the hell out of your competitors in order to win the money to eat in fine restaurants, but surrendered your stomach to a surgeon along the way, then it is obvious that you are winning for the wrong reasons—and, in reality, losing.

The pursuit of "victory" should be, I think, riveting, demanding, and, most of all, *fun*. If it isn't fun, then we might be better off losing. If you doubt this then look at one of those "successful" automatons compelled to hide an anguished psyche behind a mask of hyperactivity, pomposity, anger, and antacid. Poor devil. Locked in a trap of his own making, he's terrified to let anyone get close in case they discover the vacuum behind the glazed gaze. Way down deep he senses that something is seriously wrong, but he can't figure out what, and so he never knows what to do about it.

What he *should* do is what we're doing here—contemplate why he *really* behaves as he does, why he continues to inflict unnecessary pain upon himself. Only from there can he set about scrapping his notions of what constitutes success, get off the treadmill of his own infantile desires, and *set about becoming an authentic person*. Only then will happiness start to overtake him.

• *"Magic" will make me happy.* A "magic" solution is any remedy that we hope will come from outside ourselves—from a rabbit's foot, a crystal ball, an astrological chart, a political manifesto, a controlled substance, or a bottle. All of these things promise magic solutions. None of them work. They fail because all ''magical'' beliefs are essentially infantile. To believe in magic is to be deluded that the world can be changed as magically as it seemed to be when you were lying in that crib, and yelled, and Mommy came running. To seek magic solutions is to chase rainbows in the hope of finding wizards. *We must perform our own magic.* And we can. We do it by refusing to believe in magic, and relying upon ourselves instead.

Belief in *any* kind of magic solution is a clear sign that you are deep in the Judas Trap. And if you are caught in the Judas Trap there *cannot* be any external solution to your problems, magic or otherwise, because the core of the problem exists in your psyche.

The moral in everything I have just said is that we must make a conscious effort to reject *any* solution that comes from *outside of ourselves.* Our problems, remember, are etched into brain cells on the inside of our skulls. Hence the wisdom of Buddha: ''There is no grace, no help, to be had from the outside.''

• *A ''wizard'' will make me happy.* A wizard is a fellow who promises that *he* can work magic for you. Wizards are, as Dorothy discovered, tricksters, and nowhere is this more true than when a particular wizard believes his own pitch.

The television evangelist who promises that ''Enthooosiasm will solve orl yore problems, and faiiiiithhh will moov orl yore mount-tains'' rarely knows a goddamned thing about success in any field except the enlargement of his own glory and bank balance. He may believe his own deceits, and his sheer exuberance may buoy you for the moment. But when he leaves, where are you? You are left in a puddle of adrenaline wanting, desperately, to do something, but still not knowing what.

These kinds of people—street corner gurus and assorted "success" peddlers—are like the Wizard of Oz, tugging at *your* internal controls in order to project an image of *themselves* that is larger than life. Their illusions enthrall the child in us—the dependent child that needs to believe in magic. But this kind of magic fades the moment we reenter the real world.

The magic fades because it is *childish*. And, because it *is* childish, it is also self-defeating. We are left fluttering between elation and despair. Elation because the wizard has promised magic solutions to our problems. Despair because he has left us even more dependent than he found us. Big Daddy has gone off to charm another hall full of children who never grew up. Now *we* are alone yet again, and the world is as problematical and frightening as ever it was. And I think I hear the wicked witch coming again. Who will save me? How will I ever get to Oz now? Help!

Relax, my friend, for the help you need is close at hand.

14. *Depend on Yourself*

By endeavor, diligence, and self mastery,
let the wise man make of himself an island
that no flood can overwhelm.
BUDDHA

ON THE RAW, COLD, SIXTH DAY OF 1791'S DECEMBER, a third-class burial service was held, and a young man's body consigned to a pauper's grave. Only the grave-digger came to the burial. No tombstone or cross marked the grave. Now, no one knows where it was.

That lost grave harbors the dust of Wolfgang Amadeus Mozart. He was a genius from infancy, and his ability to play the harpsichord was declared divine. When the boy composed music, it seemed as if God were writing.

The divinity of this "radiant angel," as he was called, seemed confirmed by a feat he performed at Rome during Holy Week. Each year the *Misere* of Gregorio Allegri was performed by the papal choir. A papal decree forbade its performance anywhere else, and the only existing copy of the work was jealously guarded—any attempt to reproduce it was punishable by excommunication. Mozart heard the performance twice, then, in the privacy of his rooms, wrote down the entire complex contrapuntal score from memory. When the pope heard of this incredible achievement he awarded the boy the cross of the Order of the Golden Spur.

And so the child became the musical wonder of the age, the favorite of the Viennese court, and the apple of the Austrian emperor's eye.

Unfortunately, as the angel became a young man his mortality became increasingly apparent, and, in consequence, Mozart failed to retain the fascination of either the emperor or his court. Musicians of the day assumed that a person of Mozart's genius would be appointed court musician, but the elevation was long in coming. When it finally arrived, the emperor, like so many rich men who imagine themselves to be generous, more than lived up to his reputation for niggardliness. He slashed Mozart's miserable stipend by more than half, leaving him with less than a living wage.

Mozart became ill as well as poor, and to pay his way he did the only thing he knew: composed music. It continued to thrill the greatest minds of the age, but the general public, always fickle, lost interest in this all too perfect work. Mozart now composed letters to his friends in which he literally begged for money. He received little.

Penniless and by then critically ill, in a desperate attempt to earn the money to buy back his health,

Mozart finally embarked upon a musical race with death. In the last months of his life he wrote his three greatest symphonies, a musical mass, and an opera.

That opera, *The Magic Flute,* was his last best hope, and, in fact, after a quiet debut, it became a great musical and financial success. Pain-wracked and bedridden, Mozart would sometimes hold his watch and point out to his friends the exact moment when one of his favorite arias from this opera was being sung in the theater. The producer of the opera, however, cheated Mozart out of his royalties.

Mozart knew, in all, only thirty-five winters before he died, but his music is as vital as ever, and his place in the musical firmament seems assured. The tragedy, of course, is that he deserved so much more, and that he could have produced so much more. At the time, however, no one of sufficient influence cared enough to try to save him.

All of which brings us, dear reader, to this vital question:

If no one saved Mozart, who will save *you?*

The answer, of course, is that no one will. We must save ourselves. Buddha saw this very clearly. "Work out your own salvation," he said. "Do not depend on others." Leaning too long upon a crutch is crippling. So, too, is leaning upon other people. Our faculties wither, and we become financial, intellectual, and emotional cripples, unable either to pay, to think, or to fend for ourselves. Let's take a quick look at these aspects of dependency.

• *Financial Dependency.* An out-of-work school-teacher applying for a job in the Deep South of America was being interviewed by the school's board of governors. "Do you teach that God created man?" asked the crusty chairman. "Or do you teach the Darwinian theory of evolution?"

"Oh, er, um . . . I can teach it both ways," replied the needy teacher.

Being short of money can make us bite our tongues. Equally to the point, however, without money we may be compelled to think only what we have been paid to think. We may, soon enough, lose the faculty of thinking, and be rendered unable to *have* thoughts of our own.

Having to depend upon the goodwill of others is never wise. King Lear, thinking he could depend upon the love of his own daughters, gave them all his wealth. The money had hardly changed hands, however, than they perceived him in another light, and tossed him out into the cold.

Buddha, a prince himself, but as pragmatic as he was wise, saw clearly that, in order to survive, the man in the street needs money. Accordingly, Buddha shrewdly counseled a disciple to disperse his money thus: "Spend a quarter on your daily needs, save a quarter, and invest the rest in your business."

In itself, money cannot, of course, make anyone

happy. Conversely, while we depend upon others to finance us, we cannot even be certain of the "right" to pursue our own happiness, or even to express our own thoughts—as any organization man will tell you.

• *Intellectual Dependency.* The ability to reason separates man from the animals, yet the ability to think logically is not innate—in fact, few people are actually capable of truly logical thought. In consequence, most of us are compelled to "live" according to archaic or inane "belief systems." As a result, even when we think we're thinking, we are, for the most part, merely rearranging our prejudices—which, of course, puts us very much at the mercy of those who *can* think rationally. Little wonder, then, that we live in a society where the consumer is servant, and the adman king.

• *Emotional Dependency.* Emotional dependency reflects an unconscious wish to return to childhood. It also means addiction to childish habits: attention-getting behavior, desperate competitiveness, mindless conformity, and, one way or another, having to be looked after. Emotional dependence emasculates innate survival skills, and forces its victims to rely upon others for virtually everything: applause, opinions, goodwill, and, of course, money.

Emotional dependence was at the heart of Mozart's tragedy. As a child he was denied contact with harsh reality, and pampered without thought for his own ultimate well-being. "You are a little sorcerer," said the emperor to the long-haired boy in silk hose and puff-sleeved velvet jacket. The little sorcerer lay, at that moment, in the arms of the empress, who fondled him as though he were a doll. Only Madame Pompadour appeared aloof. When she turned her face away at his effort to kiss her, Mozart exclaimed, "Who is this that will not kiss me, when even my Empress kisses me?"

No one, unfortunately, told Mozart that the kissing would ever stop. It must have seemed to the boy who was called "God's own musical instrument" that life on earth was heaven, and, accordingly, he developed but one aspect of his personality.

Only at age twenty-seven did he venture into the world to fend for himself. At that time, Baron von Grimm, once so effusive in his praises, now observed that Mozart was "too confident, too little a man of action, too much ready to succumb to his own illusions, too little *au courant,* with the ways that lead to success."

The golden-haired boy had become a musical god, but had remained an emotional Peter Pan. He just never grew up.

He remained the child in the empress's arms, always laughed, always looked for the bright side, always believed that the heaven of his childhood would return, if only he could strike the right chord. He was depending on that. It was not enough.

RIDDING YOURSELF OF DEPENDENCY

Escaping the habit of dependency takes time, effort, and a good deal of courage. The rewards of self-reliance, however, vastly outweigh the price of achieving it. Here, if you'd like to make the effort, is a seven-step prescription to help you at least begin to make yourself less dependent.

● *Save some money.* An independent income, as Buddha was quick to point out, is worth planning for. If you weren't born rich, then one of the best ways to attain independence is to save as much as possible as fast as possible from the income that you earn. Some people call this "rainy day money." I prefer to call it "Go Jump" money. The aim is to squirrel away your money while working with an enlightened employer—someone who wants a colleague, not a servant. If you're *not* working in such a climate, then, just as soon as you've secured enough "go jump" money, tell your employer to do just that, and move onto a greener pasture. Money alone won't get you out of the Judas Trap, of course. Your "go jump" money will, however, at least afford you the opportunity to start choosing your own best interests.

● *Learn to think for yourself.* We cannot behave rationally until we learn to think clearly. This requires freeing oneself from internal and external demons by being able to examine all situations in the light of the rational facts; and then actually choosing one's own true best interests. This is easy to say, less easy to do. Encouragement to keep trying may lie in the fact that it is *impossible* to make rational choices until you realize how you are being manipulated by your own unconscious.

A short course in logic, diligently pursued, can be the beginning of intellectual independence, especially if followed by the systematic acquisition of knowledge— not knowledge of beliefs, mind you, but of facts. Armed with logic and enough facts, we can apply what we have learned and start thinking for ourselves. This will probably entail not being quite so sure of one's opinions, but that, of course, could also represent a giant step in the right direction.

• *Spot your emotional dependencies.* We hide our dependencies from everyone, ourselves included, but we cannot dodge the pain they cause us. The warning signals include headaches and heartaches, migraines and ulcers, anxiety and angst—virtually *all* emotional aches and pains portend emotional dependency. The paradox of dependency is that pain is the price we pay for what we get "for nothing." But why do we make ourselves pay this price? For the payoff, of course. But what payoff?

• *Analyze the payoff.* Until we identify the true source of our destructive behavior, we are compelled to repeat it. Therefore, in order to escape the quicksand of unconscious habit, we must *consciously* identify its cause. One way or another our bizarre behavior has its rewards. We like the sympathy, or the limelight, or we make ourselves lose in order to please a parent who didn't like to see us win, or we have some other such ghost to get even with.

• *See the futility of emotional dependence.* The

prime cure for emotional dependence lies in realizing the true nature of the problems it causes. If the Big Shot, for example, could ever *realize* how much needless suffering he is causing himself, then he would want to stop doing so immediately. That would be the beginning of developing self-reliance, and, thereby, the competency to actually *do* the job.

His other option is to realize that his prime reason for wanting the limelight—for wanting to be on the potty—is that he wants Mommy to watch him. Mommy's gone now, of course, but someone else has taken over from her—in his mind, anyway. If the poor fellow could realize that the person he's really trying to impress has ceased to exist, then he'd want the straining to stop. The realization that his behavior is both childish and destructive might then lead to the most mature decision he ever made: that there are a lot more things to life than looking like a big shot. He might realize that what he really needs, more than all of the executive suites, limousines, and private jets in the world, is *a mind of his own*.

● *Get into a new intentionality.* An "intentionality" is a state of mind that changes from the center out. When our wants are based upon conscious, autonomous, rational decisions, we change our "inner wish," and, with it, the whole mode of our being. Then, making the effort to get what we want ceases to be a problem. We stop fighting within ourselves and start to harness our own strengths. In consequence, we lose the need for "will power" to cure dependency. In fact, even to think in terms of will power is to remain caught in a bind, because we can never *force* ourselves to become self-reliant. And, thankfully, there is no need to.

Let me cite an example. When I first went to college there always seemed to be more important things than studying, and so I failed in my examinations. As a result I developed a technique for passing exams that never let me down. Whenever I didn't feel like working I formed a mental picture: I imagined that the examination results had been posted and that I had failed. I saw in my mind the faces of my friends—plus a couple of enemies. Their faces told me they had all passed. I saw my own face, too, and it was glum indeed. Then I formed a second mental picture: this time when the results were posted I had passed. People were congratulating me, slapping me on the back. I felt good.

You can see that this exercise caused a change of intentionality. I didn't have to push myself to do anything. What was previously a struggle was now almost a pleasure. And, somehow, without a lot of effort, everything seemed to get done.

• *Develop the habit of self-reliance.* The other side of dependency is self-reliance. The self-reliant person is like a fine swordsman whose primary weapon in life's battles is his skill. He doesn't waste time and energy agonizing over which stroke he will use when. Instead, he enters the fray with confidence, and parries by reflex, according to the dictate of the moment. He knows that his skill is both his weapon and his armor—and that victory depends upon his hands, his head, and, most of all, his heart. For emotional self-reliance is courage, and, therefore, also a product of practice. So the swordsman practices and becomes fully self-reliant, until, for him, the the battle of life becomes a game.

Fulfillment follows the inner resolution to take charge of our own lives, and then *following through*— actually going out and doing the job. To begin a task in this frame of mind is to conjure wizards of one's own. It is to see the task through adult eyes, and to tackle it with adult emotions. Suddenly, a powerful ally with your very best interests is at hand—*yourself*.

There is a bonus in every situation that you decide to tackle alone. Let me explain.

When I first wrote a book I was assigned an editor. As I worked on one of the early chapters I seemed to be getting nowhere, and could see no way out. So I called my editor. He had gone away for two weeks, and could not be reached. (I see now that he must have known a thing or two about the dependencies for which authors are notorious.) So, with a deadline to meet, I looked at my material again—this time, however, knowing I would have to depend entirely upon my own resources. Two days later I had it done. Once again I had been taught the value of having to depend upon myself. It showed me that I *could* do the job myself. Also, doing the job myself developed not one but *two* strengths: my technical writing skills, and the habit of emotional self-reliance.

15. *Make Changes in Your Life*

> *Any change, even a change for the better,*
> *is always accompanied by*
> *drawbacks and discomforts.*
> ARNOLD BENNETT

THE FASTEST WAY to get the kinks out of the hose is to turn on the water. So, too, one fast way out of the Judas Trap is to actually make major changes in our lives, thereby applying the kind of pressure that, like it or not, changes *us,* too, thereby bringing true "free will" into our lives.

Few people ever realize that *acquiring "free will" involves a continuing process.* Only *after* learning to play a musical instrument, for example, can I truly *choose* to play—and, even then, *what* I can choose to play will depend upon how much, and how well, I have learned. So, if I want to be able to play like an angel, I must be prepared to practice like hell.

The point is that external changes force internal changes; that *changing the way we live also changes the way we think.* External changes *compel* the brain to create new ''preferred pathways,'' thereby creating a free will that did not previously exist for us.

How do you change the way you live? There are basically four methods: by redefining your psychic contract, by putting yourself into ''sink or swim'' situations, by embarking upon graduated learning programs, and by adopting new ways of tackling old problems.

Before we do anything else, however, let's just take one last brief look at your psychic contract.

SCRAPPING YOUR PSYCHIC CONTRACT

Your psychic contract is, in essence, an unconscious understanding established early in your life with and by your parents, as to what you *ought* to do the rest of your time on earth. The psychic contract is thus a programmed agreement that denies us free will, makes us do foolish things, and turns us into so-called winners, losers, and at-leasters. What we should *really* be doing, of course, is becoming our own true selves. We cannot do that, however, until we scrap the psychic contract and stop trying to please other people—and particularly those who no longer exist.

If James Forrestal, Junior, had been able to do this, he would not have felt compelled to hang himself. If Emperor Malcolm had been able to decide that he didn't *have* to be a ''success,'' then he might have been able to actually enjoy his life. Oscar Wilde could have chosen *not* to sue the marquis. Ernest Hemingway could have stopped beating his chest. Richard Nixon could have chosen either to stop telling lies, or start burning those tapes. Judas could have stayed to finish his supper.

This whole book is, in fact, about psychic contracts, about freeing ourselves of any obligation to live our lives according to other people's programs, and, instead, responding spontaneously to life itself.

Scrapping the psychic contract is, of course, as we've seen, very much more easily said than done, and, however smart we may be, insight without action is not enough; we must also change the substance of our daily lives. Here, then, are ten specific ways in which to do that:

• *Limit association with people or organizations that have a vested interest in lowering your consciousness— and the power to do so.* The need to "win" others to our "point of view" is a fairly normal failing. Many people, on the other hand, have such a desperate need for "something to believe in," and are so blind to reality that they will believe almost anything.

Many father figures, exploiting this situation, gather thoughtless disciples and make a living (amongst other things) out of them. The problem for the leader, of course, is to keep his flock from discovering any truth except his. So, to make a profit and stay in the black, the prophet must ensure that his disciples, like mushrooms, are raised in the dark—and fed on feces.

Thus the exploitation of the "Reverend" Jim Jones's disciples involved having them flown to a faraway place and put to work building a "commune," the proceeds of which, in best *Animal Farm* tradition, went to feed the Napoleon, the pig. When reality closed in, however, it was not a matter of sending Boxer, the horse, to the glue factory, but of leading all the lambs to the slaughter.

What we can lose sight of, however, is that this whole process is a matter of degree. Most of us see through as blatantly obvious a charlatan as Jim Jones. Fewer among us, however, realize the extent to which many organizations (and their leaders) want to narrow our consciousness, thereby preserving the status quo that bests serves *their* particular interests.

Sophisticated people expect religious and political groups to lower consciousness. Less obvious, however, is the fact that many corporate empires are staffed by automatons whose leaders regard a raised consciousness as a "radical leaning"—something akin to wearing green battle fatigues in the boardroom.

Scholars and scientists can get caught in this syndrome too, for, "to get ahead," they may have to push their own particular ideas at the expense of the truth. Freud had a psychic stake in his ideas, turned them into dogma, and labeled some of his freer-thinking colleagues "deviant." This same rigidity still characterizes some members of the Freudian school.

The moral, then, is to exorcise anyone—employer, minister, mentor, educator, parent, idol, friend, partner, spouse—with any motive to put you in the dark, or keep you there. One good way to cure the problem is to re-educate the person, so you might consider giving him this book. (You might, in fact, remember Freud's dictum that his fee was a vital part of the patient's treatment, so it might be better to get your friend to buy a copy.)

• *Seek a new "cultural overlay."* Taking Judas out of his environment and putting him on, say, a Club Med cruise, would certainly have forced him to question his thinking, for nothing breaks down our preconceptions more quickly than having to survive a new or foreign culture. Mere survival forces changes in our thinking, and we quickly discover that our back-home ways are far from sacred. We temper our opinions, become more malleable, open ourselves to our new experience.

If you can't relocate abroad, then you might consider another city, or, failing that, a new suburb. Most people really could do that, and it might turn out to be quite a marked change.

• *Take a new job.* Thinking they can divorce themselves from the work they perform, some people refer to a job as "just a living," or they talk about their "performance." In fact, this performance *is* life itself. Our occupation is our prime mode of self-expression, and, accordingly, the role we choose defines our thoughts, words, acquaintances, and place in society. Ultimately, like it or not, *we become what we do.*

Buddha, an extremely smart and *realistic* fellow in almost every respect, attached great weight to the choice of a career, going so far as to make the "right occupation" a prime and fundamental step in his "noble eightfold path to enlightenment."

For what it's worth, my own advice is that all callings can be great if greatly pursued, and you should do your darnedest to make a career of something that is both enjoyable and challenging. Then your work becomes a source, not only of sustenance and pleasure, but of continuing renewal.

If, however, after giving your best, you find yourself in a job you don't enjoy, then don't waste time. Move on and do something *new* with your life. If a new job is the right job, it's also a new *life*. Use that as your criteria in job-hunting.

• *Change your beliefs.* Would you choose a car without comparing brands? No, of course not. Yet, when it comes to choosing a set of ideals, most people get stuck with the first ideology to which they were exposed.

I'd like to suggest that you live by a code of rationality. Doing that, however, might entail scrapping some old beliefs, and, depending upon how deeply you are caught in the Judas Trap, you may neither want, nor be able, to do that. As an interim measure, then, why not visit the headquarters of a few religious or political organizations whose views you truly *detest?* This exercise may enable you to see, at first hand, that many organizations demand blind obedience—and that many sheeplike people just *love* being told what to think.

For little more than conscience money you can attend

almost any church, and they all welcome potential con-
verts. Why not, then, attend an entirely new religious or
political service every week for, say, seven weeks?

Be careful though, for, in the hands of a smart guru,
we are all more susceptible to conversion than we like to
think. So, decide in advance, no matter what anyone
says, not to commit yourself to *any* new "belief sys-
tem" until one year after your first visit.

● *Follow your heart*. This means, in essence, honing
your judgment, then relying upon it. Emerson, in his
classic essay on self-reliance, called this following "the
inner gleam," and wrote that:

> A man should learn to watch that gleam of light which
> flashes across his mind from within, more than the
> lustre of the firmament of bards and sages. Yet he
> dismisses without notice his thought, because it is
> his. In every work of genius we recognize our own
> reflected thoughts; they come back to us with a cer-
> tain alienated majesty. Great works of art have no
> more abiding lesson for us than this. They teach us to
> abide by our own spontaneous impression with good-
> natured inflexibility when the whole cry of voices is
> on the other side. Else tomorrow a stranger will say
> with masterly good sense precisely what we have
> thought and felt all the time, and we shall be forced to
> take with shame our own opinion from another.

Chinese sage Lao Tzu seems to agree in this passage:

In his every movement a man of great virtue
Follows the way and the way only.
As a thing the way is
Shadowy, indistinct.
Indistinct and shadowy,
Yet within it is an image;
Shadowy and indistinct,
Yet within it is a substance.
Dim and dark,
Yet within it is an essence.
This essence is quite genuine.

Mysticism aside, modern knowledge of the brain suggests that certain cells make up a "survival mechanism" that, functioning independently of our conscious processes, monitors our behavior. This, in fact, may be the inner gleam, or "self," of which the renowned psychologist Dr. Abraham Maslow had this to say: "We have, each of us, an essential inner nature which is intrinsic or natural. . . . The inner core is . . .weak rather than strong . . . it is easily drowned out by learning, by cultural expectations, by fear, by disapproval. . . . Authentic selfhood can be defined as being able to hear these impulse voices within oneself."

Proponents of "inner tennis," like those of Zen archery, are in agreement that, when we let "it" do the work, we survive in an almost miraculous fashion. Like all athletes, however, the Zen archer also agrees that conscious practice harnesses and hones this deeper inner force, so we must make the conscious effort in order to enhance the functioning of the inner gleam.

In essence, then, we must abide by reason, *until reason tells us to let go*. Then we should let go completely and follow our intuition—which, incidentally, the dictionary defines as being "taught from within." Freud gave similar advice. He said we should attend to minor decisions consciously. In large matters where facts are unavailable, however, he distilled his advice to three words: "Follow your heart."

• *Make time to hear yourself*. I have two suggestions. First, devote three minutes of every day to complete silence. Do nothing else at the time. Don't read, don't think, don't listen. Instead, *feel* the world turn, holding to what the Chinese call "the noble silence." Three minutes is so short a time that some people would say it's not enough. Well, it's a start, and that's critical. If you find more time, take it.

My second suggestion is that you save one day a week in which to retreat from the the outer world, and, one hopes, to thereby discover the inner gleam. Make it a quiet day without work, media jangle, or stress of any kind—a day in which to heed Albert Einstein's advice to a friend: "Rejoice with your family in the beautiful land of life."

This "day off" isn't really so much a day as a concept. And it's not, I have to confess, a new concept, but simply the Sabbath in disguise. (We need the disguise to save it from the puritans.)

Philosopher John Ruskin decided to do much the same with all his days. In a letter to a friend he said: "I'm tired of benevolence and eloquence and everything that's proper, and I'm going to cultivate myself and nobody else, and see what will come of that."

● *Till the soil in your head.* The distinguished psychologist Carl Jung had a mystical bent and endorsed the notion that, as well as hearing your own self, you can also tap a "collective unconscious."

This may or may not be so. What is true, however, is that we all have extremely easy access to the conscious thoughts of great men and women, for, although writers die, their words, fresh as the day they were penned, are lying around in books, waiting, impatiently as ever, for an audience. The same is true, of course, of music and the visual arts.

People often shy away from such pursuits, claiming they can't be bothered, or that they haven't got time, or that they can "see nothing in them." The latter is often, regrettably, literally true, the reason being that we cannot see *anything* worthwhile until we have created thinking pathways that permit us to comprehend the world before us. And that, my friend—challenging one's own mind—is both difficult to do, and challenging to begin.

What you might do, for openers, is to take out an *expensive* subscription to a monthly series of books, or musical performances, or gallery exhibitions. If you pay enough, you may feel compelled to get your money's worth. That way, you just might.

• *Change your existing environment.* This means ridding yourself of as many distractions as possible. Here are four suggestions:

1. Terminate the television. Or restrict your viewing to no more than three hours a week. That's a *lot* of time when you think how hard it is to get some people to keep a three-minute silence.
2. Remove the radio.
3. Show vexing "friends" the door. Jesus said not to "cast your pearls before swine." Buddha, though he resisted the temptation to call his detractors pigs, gave similar advice: "If, as one fares, one does not find a companion who is better or equal, let one resolutely pursue the solitary path; there can be no fellowship with the fool."
4. Curtail junk reading—until you've finished all those great books. The world will not end in the meantime, and if it does you'll probably just have time to hear the bang.

• *Pursue a new interest.* A consuming passion for the latest television sit-coms doesn't qualify. What you want is something absorbing, challenging, and, initially anyway, *difficult*—something that will tax your brain. Here are sixteen suggestions:

1. Climb a specific mountain. Start with a hill if you prefer.

149

2. Become a ranked chess player.
3. Charter a "bare-boat" yacht, and learn to sail.
4. Learn celestial navigation.
5. Learn a musical instrument.
6. Write a technical article—and get it published.
7. Write a book.
8. Learn a new language.
9. Join a public speaking club, and try to get a word in.
10. Study Oriental flower arranging.
11. Learn to program a computer.
12. Take up photography and develop your own films.
13. Learn to paint portraits in oils.
14. Learn to tap dance.
15. Go scuba diving.
16. Take a trip on a New York subway. (If you dare.)

16. *Enjoy Each Day*

A ZEN BUDDHIST, pursued by a tiger to the edge of a ravine, escapes by lowering himself on a vine hanging from the precipice. The vine sags, however, and the rocks below appear as sharp as the teeth of the tiger above. Suddenly the Buddhist sees a strawberry growing in a crevice. With one hand he plucks the strawberry and puts it upon his palate. "Ah, how sweet it is," he says.

Zen training has enabled him to see, and to savor, the moment. By contrast, most people run through life seeking its "meaning," while failing to appreciate the meaning that already exists *within everyday life*. Such people are like rodents seeking food while running through the holes in a giant Swiss cheese: they can't see the cheese for the holes.

Emulating the Zen Buddhist begins with the realization that this *one fleeting life* is all we have, or ever will have. That *this* is all there is or ever will be. That this is *not a rehearsal,* but the *real thing.* That we are living our lives—or failing to live our lives—now, right *now.* The enchanted land of Oz is all about us. Heaven is here. Nirvana is *now.*

This is it, my friend.
This is it.

The catch, of course, is that we must be able to see this for ourselves, *and then we must create whatever we want "it" to be.* Why not try to create a heaven?

HOW TO CREATE A HEAVEN

How do we create a heaven? Fortunately, the job's pretty well done. For the most part, we only have to rearrange our thinking. Here are seven things that will help us to do the job:

Accept that we are solely responsible for our own good time. Who will organize the good times if we don't do that for ourselves? Nobody will. *Nobody,* do you hear me? Nobody. If you doubt it, then think back again on Mozart's tragedy.

Consciously create a happy and fulfilling life. This means making a deliberate effort to enjoy life every day by doing such things as:

• Reading a poem or part of a novel

- Listening to—and hearing—a piece of music
- Seeking and meeting a minor challenge in one's work
- Seeing the sun come up, or go down
- Listening to—and really hearing—a friend

Add an element of ritual to your life. The American Indian added ceremony to his tobacco, thereby enhancing its flavor, and his life. We can do the same. How? There are thousands of ways but here are a few examples:

- Making an event of family mealtimes, adding candles, flowers, a glass of wine, soft music;
- Observing a friend's birthday with a card, a cake, a call;
- Setting aside an afternoon to honor the onset of each of the seasons;
- Making a special event of your own special milestones, like remembering the day you graduated from school, or got married, or moved to a new neighborhood.

Be open to spontaneous activity. The word *spontaneity* derives from the Latin *sponte,* which means "of one's own free will." To live spontaneously, therefore, is to live fully one's own life, moment by moment by moment. An automaton cannot act spontaneously because it is entranced—and entrapped—by its script.

We are all spontaneous before we become scripted. Children are receptive to love, and giving of it. In consequence they make friends easily. They are truly alive, and are, therefore, able to be totally themselves while they are playing. Adults, on the other hand, "play" complicated, joyless games. All too often, adults *cannot* enjoy themselves because they cannot *be* themselves. The roles they play are not their own.

Being ourselves *means* acting spontaneously. When we do that, when we can open up to others, we cause them, in turn, to open up to us.

Make time to play. Puritans confuse play with self-indulgence. The essence of play is to lose ourselves in pursuit of a pleasure that leaves us replenished, and, therefore, better able to work. The pleasure in play is directly related to its spontaneity, and to the extent that it "takes us out of ourselves."

Pastimes like chess, as any chess addict will tell you, are exciting because the element of spontaneity is built in. Nobody knows for sure how any game will go. Playing isn't escaping life, playing *is* life. A robot cannot truly play because it cannot respond of its own free will.

17. *The Judas Trap Dismantled and a Last Piece of Great Advice*

> *Be as careful at the end as at the beginning,*
> *And there will be no ruined enterprises.*
> LAO TZU

BEING IN THE JUDAS TRAP means thinking you're in charge of your life when, in fact, you are ensnared by scripting and a constellation of illusions that springs from dependency. The combination of these elements "preordains" your behavior and makes conscious, rational judgments impossible.

In the end, escaping the Judas Trap comes down to doing six things:

1. Reject the illusion of autonomy, thereby realizing that you're in the trap;
2. Examine your script with a view to understanding the real roots of your behavior;

155

3. Dispel illusions that spring from "childish" desires;
4. Create a new "psychic contract," choosing to live *your* life according to *your* code;
5. Make changes in your life, in order to gain control of it;
6. Live fully in the "now."

So, you don't actually *get* out of the trap, but rather you *dismantle* it. You take your old life apart, one element at a time, and then you make changes in your daily life to create a new one. It's as easy—and as difficult—as that.

At this point, let's look at one last fellow in the trap, in order to show two things: first, the subtlety, and, therefore, the power, of the trap. And, second, to permit *you* to see the way in which *your* mind can work against you.

Your reaction to this last example may tell whether you will ever escape the Judas Trap. Being able to think, rationally, about this example is a good sign. However, if your mind closes, and stays closed, then escape may be impossible. Let's look, then, and you see what you think.

THE REBEL WHO WANTED TO BE CAUGHT IN THE JUDAS TRAP

A uniquely insightful, if somewhat rebellious boy was told he was God, believed it, set out to prove it, and, in consequence, fulfilled a chilling family destiny.

This maverick fulfilled his "destiny" on two clear levels. On one level his *conscious* wish was to stay on script, and make all the minor details of his destiny, including his last words, hang together.

On the other level he was smart enough to know that he might be deluding himself. As death approached he seriously questioned his motivations in meditation. The answers, however, were already written in "prophecies" that he *wanted* to fulfill; and, even more powerfully, in the copy of these prophecies—these scripts, really—that constituted his programming.

Like Oscar Wilde, this rebel also believed that he was destined to suffer, but in this case the distress had to be terminal. So, impelled to seek his own demise, the rebel embarked upon a collision course with society, which, in accordance with his wishes, killed him.

The matter did not die there, however. In accordance with *their* scripts, the rebel's followers also believed in his deity. Accordingly, the *fact* of the death of their "indestructible" leader lay, literally, beyond their comprehension. Accordingly, they chose to believe that their ideologue had merely entered "another world."

This phenomenon—the creation of new beliefs to support discredited old beliefs—is fairly common in situations of intense stress. The inability to acknowledge the death of a loved one is, of course, an automatic reaction, and it is entirely normal in such circumstances to believe that the deceased has "gone to heaven."

Similarly, people unable to accept the fact of Adolf Hitler's death chose to believe, instead, that he had gone to Argentina.

In the case of the young rebel, however, one more psychological twist gave a special significance to the whole affair. In the moment of his death he was placed in a fortuitously symbolic position: *his head was raised higher than that of his fellows.*

The rebel in question here, Jesus of Nazareth, died high upon a cross that had been raised onto a hill. The resulting image of Jesus in the moment of his death was thus laden with immense emotional power. And, of course, it still is. Even today, as throughout time, it is impossible even to think of Jesus without "looking up."

The Christians have a more powerful father figure than any in history. Replicas of Jesus on the cross hang in churches throughout the world. The image is indelibly imprinted upon the "conscience cards" of millions, many of whom—electronic preachers, for example—have a heavy cash investment in keeping the image very high in the public mind. The result is that virtually no Christian can discuss Christianity rationally.

Add the image of Jesus in the moment of his death to his incredibly sharp insight, his belief in his own deity, the fact that he *did,* as foretold, fulfill Scripture, and you begin to appreciate why the image of Jesus is such a compelling father figure.

But, of course, another kind of death—say by stoning in a pit—would have conjured no special psychological symbolism, making Jesus' story perhaps no more than a historical footnote, and Christianity possibly just a minor cult.

Had Jesus gained access to Freud's ideas, had he known of the existence of the unconscious—and understood its power—he might well have chosen a happier fate.

In any event, in the light of Freudian insight, it seems clear that Jesus was caught in one more Judas Trap than he had been able to foresee. A web of unconscious forces, beginning with beliefs imprinted upon his brain as he lay in his crib, caused him to seek a prophetic family destiny. His demise was thus preordained only insofar as he could do nothing else at the time.

One moral of Jesus' tragedy is that even the wisest of men can fall prey to their scripting, thereby losing charge of their lives. Socrates, you may recall, also found himself in a situation calling for his premature demise, without rational cause.

Prior to Freud, only one major philosopher realized the existence—and the power—of the unconscious. Some 2,600 years ago, Buddha observed that "through ignorance are conditioned volitional actions . . . and these in turn give rise to conditioned consciousness." Armed with this understanding, Buddha rejected all illusions, went on to live a truly enlightened life, and to die of old age.

II. *Wareham's Way Out of the Judas Trap*

In the hope that you may do the same, let me leave you with one last thought:

*Live now as if you are already living a second life,
and as if you had acted in your first life
as wrongly as you are about to act now.*

BIBLIOGRAPHY

Many great works, both of fact and of fiction, are about what I have called the Judas Trap. It is, therefore, impossible to list all sources for a book such as this. Accordingly, the following is part bibliography and part suggested reading. The criteria for inclusion are that a book listed has been of help to me, and may well be of help to others. Recommended books are starred thus *. Two stars mean highly recommended.

**Berne, Eric. *Games People Play*. London: Penguin, 1971.

Berne, Eric. *Beyond Games and Scripts*. New York: Ballantine Books, 1976.

*Bettelheim, Bruno. *Freud and Man's Soul*. New York: Knopf, 1983.

Bukkyo Dendo Kyokai. *The Teaching of Buddha*. Tokyo: Buddhist Promoting Foundation, 1978.

**Beecher, Willard and Marguerite. *Beyond Success and Failure*. New York: Pocket Books, 1971.

*Campbell, H. J., Dr. *The Pleasure Areas*. New York: Ballantine Books, 1978.

Cross, Milton. *Encyclopedia of the Great Composers and Their Music*. Garden City, New York: Doubleday, 1953.

Dowling, Colette. *The Cinderella Complex*. New York: Pocket Books, 1981.

Dunne, Carrin. *Buddha and Jesus*. Springfield, Illinois: Templegate Publishers, 1975.

*Epstein, Joseph. *Ambition: The Secret Passion*. New York: Dutton, 1980.

**Frankl, Victor E. *Man's Search for Meaning*. New York: Pocket Books, 1963.

Freud, Sigmund. *Introductory Lectures on Psychoanalysis*. New York: W. W. Norton & Co., 1977.

*Fromm, Erich. *Escape from Freedom*. New York: Avon Books, 1965.

Fromm, Erich. *Greatness and Limitations of Freud's Thought*. New York: Mentor Book, 1981.

Bibliography

Fromm, Erich. *Psychoanalysis and Religion*. New Haven: Yale University Press, 1959.

**Fromm, Erich. *To Have or To Be*. New York: Bantam Books, 1981.

*Hall, Edward T. *Beyond Culture*. New York: Anchor Press-Doubleday, 1977.

Herrigel, Eugen. *Zen in the Art of Archery*. New York: Vintage Books, 1971.

Hofstadter, Douglas R. *Gödel, Escher, Bach: An Eternal Golden Braid*. New York: Vintage Books, 1980.

Huxley, Aldous. *Brave New World*. New York: Harper & Row, 1969.

**Jaynes, Julian. *The Origin of Consciousness in the Breakdown of the Bicameral Mind*. Boston: Houghton Mifflin Co., 1982.

Lau, D. C. *Lao Tzu Tao Te Ching*. London: Penguin Books, 1963.

Maslow, Abraham H. *Toward a Psychology of Being*. New York: D. Van Nostrand Co., 1968.

May, Rollo. *Freedom and Destiny*. New York: W. W. Norton and Co., 1981.

May, Rollo. *Love and Will*. New York: Dell, 1969.

May, Rollo. *The Meaning of Anxiety*. New York: Pocket Books, 1979.

Newman, M., and Berkowitz, B. *How to Be Your Own Best Friend*. New York: Ballantine Books, 1974.

Pearson, Hesketh. *The Life of Oscar Wilde*. London: Macdonald & Jane's, 1975.

**Prochnik, Leon. *Endings*. New York: Crown Publishers, 1980.

Rahula, Walpola. *What the Buddha Taught*. New York: Grove Press, 1974.

*Rogers, Carl R. *On Becoming a Person*. Boston: Houghton Mifflin Co., 1961.

*Sheehy, Gail. *Passages*. New York: Bantam Books, 1977.

Skinner, B. F. *Beyond Freedom and Dignity*. Harmondsworth, England: Penguin, 1973.

Russell, Bertrand. *Why I Am Not a Christian*. New York: Simon & Schuster, 1957.

Steiner, M. Claude. *Scripts People Live*. New York: Bantam Books, 1974.

Suzuki, D. T. *An Introduction to Zen Buddhism*. New York: Grove Press, 1964.

*Terkel, Studs. *Working*. New York: Avon Books, 1975.

Tillich, Paul. *The Courage To Be*. New Haven: Yale University Press, 1952.

Wareham, John R. *Secrets of a Corporate Headhunter*. New York: Atheneum, 1980.

Watts, Alan. *This Is It*. New York: Vintage Books, 1973.

Yankelovich, Daniel. *New Rules*. New York: Bantam Books, 1982.

John Wareham was born in New Zealand, where he attended Victoria University of Wellington, graduated with a bachelor of commerce degree, and qualified both as a chartered accountant and an economist.

He founded Wareham Associates, an executive search and appraisal firm in 1964, and has since extended its operations to encompass eight offices on three continents, with headquarters in New York.

Having devoted nearly half a lifetime to researching and appraising executive behavior, John Wareham has become a foremost authority upon the subject. Many of his methods have become touchstones of personnel practice. His last book, *Secrets of a Corporate Headhunter*, is widely regarded as an indispensable and classic guide to the human side of management.

John Wareham is an active squash player, a yachtsman of some distinction, and an accomplished public speaker. His spare-time interests also include opera, ballet, drama, and music.